HAUNTED
ST. AUGUSTINE AND
ST. JOHNS COUNTY

ELIZABETH RANDALL
PHOTOGRAPHY BY BOB RANDALL

Haunted
America

Published by Haunted America
A Division of The History Press
Charleston, SC 29403
www.historypress.net

Copyright © 2013 by Elizabeth Randall
All rights reserved

First published 2013

Manufactured in the United States

ISBN 978.1.62619.226.3

Library of Congress CIP data applied for.

Notice: The information in this book is true and complete to the best of our knowledge. It is offered without guarantee on the part of the author or The History Press. The author and The History Press disclaim all liability in connection with the use of this book.

All rights reserved. No part of this book may be reproduced or transmitted in any form whatsoever without prior written permission from the publisher except in the case of brief quotations embodied in critical articles and reviews.

To our brave grandmothers, Sylvia Marilyn Peterson and Elsie Robinson Farley—two pioneering spirits whom we would love to see again.

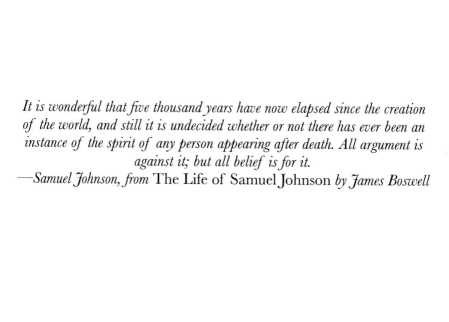

It is wonderful that five thousand years have now elapsed since the creation of the world, and still it is undecided whether or not there has ever been an instance of the spirit of any person appearing after death. All argument is against it; but all belief is for it.
—*Samuel Johnson, from* The Life of Samuel Johnson *by James Boswell*

CONTENTS

CONTENTS

FOREWORD

When Elizabeth Randall first asked me to write a foreword for her book about ghost stories, I admit there was a bit of hesitation. After all, nature and "sense of place" are more my thing as an author and as a longtime Floridian simply trying to figure out what this wacky and gorgeous and wildly misunderstood state is really about.

But Elizabeth is one of the most accomplished and clever writers I know. I immersed myself into *Haunted St. Augustine and St. Johns County* and rode with its current. When I surfaced, I had a grin on my face and a renewed sense of assurance that Florida is still one of the most singular places in all the world.

As Elizabeth has discovered, this authentically offbeat county is far more than a mood-setting backdrop for novels and films or any mainstream hype promoting theme parks and shopping malls.

Indeed, as most students of the real Florida know, the so-called Sunshine State is just about anything we imagine it to be. So, why not launch a wondrous and droll journey into "old Florida's rich culture of supernatural lore"?

Within this context, St. Johns County—home to some of our most historic settlements—is a perfectly sensible place to base a quest for our subtropical ghosts, as well as all the cold spots, chilling mists and floating orbs of protoplasm that reportedly travel with them.

Elizabeth, who readily admits to being a "ghost agnostic," gamely forges ahead into an excursion she promises will be far more organic than the staged repetition of Disney's "Haunted Mansion" ride. In doing so, she picks up the thread others have trailed through their own stories of the supernatural here—from the "unicorn" once spotted on the shores of the St. Johns River in the sixteenth century to the Gothic myths tilled by Stetson Kennedy and others in the Works Progress Administration Florida Writers Project earlier in the twentieth century.

In this way, *Haunted St. Augustine* might fit into the genre of surrealism that so often inhabits the memories, dreams and reflections of our art and literature—a model that creatively seeks "freedom from excessive rational thought." Tired of mind-numbing work behind a counter or in a cubicle? Kick back and let the spirits romp about and liven up your world for a bit.

Come along with Elizabeth—and husband photographer Bob—as they meander down this ephemeral trail of ghosts. The first thing you'll notice is that St. Johns County seems to be actively haunted. As Elizabeth has found, it's no longer enough to advertise places as simply "historic" or "old," as St. Augustine has done for years. She observes, "There's been a distinctive shift in the tourist market from places to see that are the *oldest* to places that are the most *haunted*." In St. Augustine, there are no less than a dozen tours themed to haunting, and there's also plenty of ghost-sleuthing accessories that can be used along the way. At one of the ghost hunting kiosks, Elizabeth finds a "ghost gadget used to detect cold spots left by protoplasm" that looked "amazingly like the stud-finder in Bob's toolbox at home."

Nonetheless, Elizabeth gifts each story—which is first recounted in the words of a local true believer—ample room for expression. Every tale is also accompanied by a very real history, and it is her careful recounting of that history that informs the respective stories with a wonderful Faulknerian texture. This is no less powerful than the classic nature-shape-place dynamic; it's just a bit more…creative.

As with UFOs, visitors to this ghostly shadow land are either true believers or not. But even a ghost agnostic like Elizabeth admits to being puzzled at times. During her visit to a St. Augustine antique shop that had once been a jail and drunk tank for prisoners a few centuries ago, she is told that "Pedro," the resident ghost, once darted out to catch a modern light bulb before it fell to the floor. She wonders how an inebriated ghost could be that nimble.

In this way, *Haunted St. Augustine* helps chart some delicious new territory in the realm of what might rightly be called the genre of Florida-Phantom-Heritage travel.

Bill Belleville
June 2013

PREFACE

Wits describe Florida as the "Rodney Dangerfield of the South." *We get no respect.* Our biggest claims to fame on a national scale are "hanging chads" and Casey Anthony. With education budgets shrinking, the housing market imploding and unemployment rising, we are no longer viewed as Ponce de Leon's desirable "land of flowers." Florida, in general, is viewed as the proverbial country cousin who was transformed by slick city developers with long, low cars and bags of moolah—not into Cinderella, but rather more like one of her stepsisters with lots of plastic surgery. There's plenty of smooth, stinky asphalt in place of dust, mud and toe-stubbers. The reeking mounds of landfills replace the bouquet of orange groves. The compressed years of meandering sameness, of livestock and impenetrable woodland, gone, exploded into a hurricane of shopping malls and theme parks.

Florida may be all of this to outsiders, but to the people who live here, it is altogether different. Bob and I have lived in Florida a combined total of seventy-one years. We're not natives, as few people in Florida are, but we are Floridians in the truest sense of a situational shift. We have seen Florida past and present, north and west, east and south, its swamps, its woods, its white-top beaches and its grassy waters. We have traveled the highways and byways, the sand, the muck, the cracked tarmac and the wet roads as glossy as glass gashed on either side by canals or by miles upon miles of telephone poles, rail fences and livestock munching dark blades of grass against a blood-red sunset. We have baked under its fierce sun when the air was heavy with the fragrance of magnolia and honeysuckle, we have wandered under filigree Spanish moss hanging from centurion trees and we have emerged from the ashes of the roiling fires of its sugar cane tracts. We have hunkered down in safe rooms from its mighty storms and sailed, canoed and kayaked on glittering water under immense bridges linking islands made of coral and coquina. Florida is not scenery, a backdrop or a stage for those of us who stay, and it is big enough to combine land and sea, city and country into a peninsular patchwork that is at once impenetrable and enigmatic. Florida becomes who we are and who we want to be.

But what is that exactly? Well, for one thing, Florida is a product of its history, and in terms of our book, it is old Florida's rich culture of supernatural lore. We use the word "lore" instead of "facts" for a reason. If you've been to St. Johns County in the past ten years, you've probably seen a distinctive shift in the tourist market from places to see that are the *oldest* to places to see that are the most *haunted*. Paula Crouch Thrasher in a 1998 article for the *Atlanta Journal-Constitution* wrote about St. Augustine, "Everything old is revered here. There's the Old Market at the Plaza, the Oldest House, the Oldest Wooden Schoolhouse, the Oldest Drugstore, the Oldest Store Museum, the Oldest Jail." Now, fifteen years later, St. Augustine boasts at least a dozen different kinds of ghost tours including our favorite, GhoST. Augustine.

In many tourist cities in Florida, there are haunted pub tours, haunted carriage rides, ghost train adventures and ghost cruises. Bob and I have been on more than a few of these. Our guides would nudge us toward "cold spots," analyze every breeze, encourage us to take pictures of floating orbs and explain ruefully that the actual ghost sighting or apparition or EVP (electronic voice phenomenon) was *last* night or *yesterday*'s ghost tour or maybe tomorrow's if we want to come back. Local stores set up ghost cams, an infrared camera used to detect "mists" and "full-body apparitions." At one of the ghost hunting kiosks, a ghost gadget used to detect cold spots left by protoplasm looked amazingly like the stud-finder in Bob's toolbox at home.

Yet we also talked to many sincere people in St. Augustine who recounted incredible stories of ghostly legend and happenstance that they actually experienced or accrued from an accountable source.

All of this is really a prelude to a confession that may sound odd coming from a couple of people who have spent over a year chasing, photographing and writing about paranormal sightings in historic places up and down Florida's northeast coast. But the confession is this: Bob and I have never seen a ghost. We have never seen an orb that couldn't be explained by a trick of light, a mist that wasn't accountable to actual water vapor, a voice, a creak, a sound or anything at all resembling the occult, the supernatural and the paranormal. It's not that we were skeptical either. We were dying, if you'll pardon the pun, to see something authentic from some other dimension. Although we did have a few odd experiences, we experienced absolutely nothing that would qualify us to become what insiders in paranormal research like to call "believers." Which is not to say that we don't believe. Bob and I like to refer to ourselves as "ghost agnostics."

Instead, what we have gained from this research is a series of adventures that bound us even closer to our home state and the discovery of a part of the state that, despite our long tenure, we really knew little about. We learned a lot about St. Johns' fascinating history, which weaved and overlapped from one place to another. The haunted places we describe in this book will appeal to native Floridians and to nomadic tourists who have more than theme parks in mind. In fact, we like to think of it as a "historic haunted trail," enabling travel to each site in a logical sequence from a variety of vantage points. Our book is also a "supernatural" source of documentation for leagues of tourists who want more than Disney's "Haunted Mansion" and wish to begin an adventure in search of haunted St. Johns County.

Along the way, we have relived history and pored over lists, records, documents, books, letters and maps. In St. Augustine, we found out why the little boy ghost, Jamie Morgan, frequently sighted in a St. Augustine cemetery, is so lonely, and we recounted a ghastly murder that still haunts a family plot. Forts, a jail, bars, a lighthouse, restaurants, a hotel, a college, an old drugstore and more also make up some of the stories in this book of haunted places.

We have found that there was a ghost story behind every historic building and place, but the ghost was not the whole story. Sharing tales of the past kept the history from getting lost. As Tom Shroder, a former editor of the *Washington Post*, put it, "Narrative is the way that human beings are genetically coded to understand the world." There is a story behind everything: how a bridge was named, why a city grew here and not there, even the landscape of a terrestrial hammock. Ghost stories provide an echo, a persistence of relevance after the people and the events that affected a place are long gone.

Believer or not, you will hear that echo when you visit the haunted places of St. Johns County.

ACKNOWLEDGEMENTS

S pecial thanks to our daughter, Courtney Randall, who ate chicken potpies while we were on the road; our granddaughter, Cassidy Jasmann, who offered her encouragement; and our friend and mentor Bill Belleville, who gave us direction. Thanks also to Jack Bass for his enormous reservoir of knowledge about Florida byways and waterways. Of immense help was Charley Tingley of the St. Augustine Historical Society. Thanks also to Peter Gold of St. Augustine Gold Tours. I would also like to thank the wonderful people of St. Johns County who answered my many questions and welcomed me as one of their own.

Introduction

Like many northeast Florida counties, St. Johns County was occupied by more than one distinct territorial flag. Spain, Britain and the United States have all lent their influence to the culture, architecture and history of the huge county situated between the Atlantic Ocean and the St. Johns River.

The county used to be much larger. When Juan Ponce de Leon landed in St. Johns County in 1513, he claimed all of Florida east of the Suwannee River. Since then, St. Johns County has the dubious distinction of being the first and the last Florida County, other than Volusia, to actually cede land to create other counties — land that is now part of Flagler, Duval, Alachua and Nassau Counties.

Settled as the first established European colony in 1565 by Admiral Pedro Menéndez Aviles, St. Augustine was occupied by Spain until 1763, when Britain finally acquired it after decades of bloody battles. The British flag flew from Castillo de San Marcos (renamed Fort Marion during this period) for only two decades. Then Spain retook it as the prize for its alliance with Americans during the Revolutionary War.

In the lull between occupations, William Bartram, the famed eighteenth-century travel writer and environmentalist, snaked a trail through St. Johns County.

The second Spanish period of St. Johns County was less auspicious than the first. Some of the original settlers returned from Cuba, where they'd been exiled, but many did not, most notably the freed slaves from the first established black community in North America: the Fort Mose settlement.

Low on money and manpower and at war with France, Spain relinquished the territory to the United States in 1819. It took the United States two years to hoist the Stars and Stripes over St. Johns County.

Unfortunately, 1821 was the year the St. Augustine population was disseminated by the plague of yellow fever. Because of its deep harbors, St. Johns County picked up trade with other countries. This yielded luxuries but also introduced disease, most notably quarantines of yellow fever, which cut back on St. Johns County's most profitable economic draw: tourism. The discovery by Dr. Walter Reed that yellow fever's viral origin was mosquito-borne was a godsend to the coastal communities in Florida, but it didn't occur until the twentieth century.

During its American occupation, St. Johns County also endured the plague of two wars: the Second Seminole War and the Civil War, when Union troops occupied most of northeastern Florida. The population of St. Johns County was divided on allegiance in the War Between the States; Union and Confederate sympathizers lived, worked and brawled side by side. It wasn't the last time St. Johns County would be divided because of human rights.

St. Johns County's involvement in the civil rights movement of the 1960s was famous and infamous. Sit-ins, marches down King Street, boycotts, arrests and altercations were all part of the local landscape played out on a national stage. Martin Luther King Jr. visited the city, but local hotels operated under Jim Crow laws. He was arrested during a demonstration and spent the night in the St. Augustine jail. Further outrages and excesses of St. Augustine segregationists were reported in newspapers and on TV throughout the world. For that reason, some historians credit St. Johns County civil rights activists for bringing the issue to national attention, which led to the Civil Rights Act of 1964.

Still the center of community activism today, St. Augustine and St. Augustine Beach are the most densely populated tourist spots in St. Johns County, while the communities of Ponte Verda, Elkton, Hastings and Fruit Cove are well known to locals. St. George Street in St. Augustine composes the historic district of St. Johns County. Some of the historic buildings in this area are authentic, and some are reconstructed to a greater or a lesser degree.

The intercoastal region features mangroves, salt marshes, shrimp and blue crab, but it is the coquina rock compositions, evident along the barrier islands in southern St. Johns County, that supplied the materials for construction. Coquina, indigenous to the region, was used to build many of the historic sites of St. Johns County, including the Castillo de San Marcos.

Rich in history, resources and entertainment, St. Johns County has some of the best weather in Florida. Almost every day is hot and sunny, and it rarely rains. Designated in 2000, the St. Johns River is one of only fourteen in the United States as an American Heritage River for its cultural and ecological values. Yet the lifeblood of St. Johns County resides primarily in its most famous and its oldest city.

The year 2013 is a banner one for St. Augustine, celebrating five hundred years since its European discovery by Juan Ponce de Leon. There is a statue of the famed explorer in the Plaza de la Constitucion, which coincidentally is the heart of the city of St. Augustine.

From here, the Bridge of Lions is visible—that and the endless stream of cars with out-of-state plates. On warm evenings in the summer, it is still light out at 8:30 p.m., and dozens of people congregate at the north end, which is across the street from the Cathedral of Basilica St. Augustine. On the other side of the plaza, residents gather on lawn chairs, drinking bottled water and listening to a local band. And there they all are: people and tourists stationed on separate sides of the plaza but still, for all intents and purposes, on common ground.

The plaza is the place where visitors and the local community converge. It's easy to tell them apart in St. Augustine. For one thing, the tourists travel in packs. For another, there are more of them. On St. George Street, they consult maps and then walk quickly to congregate in throngs on the corner of Cathedral Place for a trolley tour or a ghost tour. A man and his son walk by a sign proclaiming events in the plaza sponsored by, among others, St. Johns County Tourist Development Council. The boy asks, "Are we going to a concert, Daddy?" A few feet away, a man kneels in the grass, pointing a camera at a beautiful woman who poses under a tree, her arms around two adorable children. A girl walks across the Plaza de la Constitucion carrying two boxes of takeout pizza.

St. Augustine is a little like Europe, with tiendas del café, where patrons are welcome to sit, read, write or tap on a laptop. Florida tourists arrive, too, coming through to enjoy the ambiance. Or perhaps they are off to the Hotel Casa Monica for a drink or for its eclectic air-conditioned art gallery.

A cathedral can take nine hundred years to finish. Masons would never see the fruits of their toil, but they were building toward the future. Like the masons, many of St. Johns County's citizens propose creative ideas to build a future. They're involved in local government. They organize food banks for the homeless. They preserve their precious environment.

The lifeblood of the county of St. Johns is the city of St. Augustine, and the heart of St. Augustine is its people. But a heart is only a vessel. It is a huge, hollow cavity that cannot break; it can only contract and expand. Yes, modern development will always encroach upon Florida, but in St. Johns County and its outlying areas, there is still plenty of natural beauty, historic sites and mystery to uncover from the past, the present and the future.

ANTIQUES & UNIQUES COLLECTIBLES

THE OLD CITY JAIL

We do not send alcoholics to jail in this country.
—*Ralph Nader,* New York Times, *2000*

Close to the Spanish Military Hospital is a flat-roofed, two-story antique store with a balcony and a decorative railing.

Tourists going into Larry Altman's Antiques & Uniques Collectibles may notice a monitor set up by the cash register. Armstrong is not checking out shoplifters. Since this is St. Augustine, the screen is, naturally, a ghost cam intended to catch mists, apparitions, shadows, fluorescent light and all the paranormal things that St. Augustine merchants encounter, or hope to encounter, in order to boost tourist trade.

Armstrong has organized something called the Ancient Aviles Ghost Trek; for a fee, paranormal investigators make reservations to set up their equipment in his shop to record and film ghosts. According to Armstrong, some "pending television" deals were forthcoming.

Why would ghost hunters want to stake out an antique store? "It was the city jail," Armstrong explains, "from 1888 to 1893. Just two cells, in the back there." He waves in the direction of the room customers regularly peruse for antique bookends. Armstrong also has a ghost story to tell:

> *Look at that florescent fixture there. If you look at the spring-loaded end, you see that I have electrical tape on it. What happened was, I was sitting on the other side of the counter, and my wife was in the back. All of a*

Above: Reconstructed storefront of the Old City Jail.

Left: Exhibit of bizarre collectibles.

sudden, there was a loud crash. The big light had just burned through the base. The bulb came out. That bulb hit the top of one of these metal racks that was at the end of the counter. Smashed into it. Knocked over some pictures that were on top. Continued on to the other side of the shop. Slammed into a shelf and broke a couple of the shot glasses. Continued on. The bulb ended up on a rack on the second shelf on the same side of the room where it originally fell. Didn't shatter. Now, it's obvious why it came out. Why it didn't break is the question. My wife, she's very, very sensitive, so based on conversations and readings, she thinks a person named "Pedro" took the bulb as it fell and put it back.

THEN AND NOW

According to Charles Tingley, archivist and historian of the St. Augustine Historical Society and research library, Armstrong was right about the building.

"It was actually a city drunk tank," Tingley said, "a one-story holding cell made of poured concrete after the 1887 fire. If you go around to the side, you can see the portions of brick and concrete where they added on." The jail was vacated in 1893 and enlarged in 1899 when two stories were added to the front of the original structure.

Then, in the early twentieth century, it was made into a Chinese laundry—the only Chinese business in town. It was a fishing tackle shop for about thirty years and then an art gallery. It was owned by a friend of Tingley's, Theador Weber, a decorated World War II army veteran, who rented out the space until he died in 1995.

Named for the founder of St. Augustine, Pedro Menéndez de Aviles, the narrow cobblestone street where Antiques & Uniques Collectibles resides was once the center of the old Spanish quarter, settled in 1565. Continuously occupied since then, it hosts a large number of buildings ranging from colonial to modern architecture. A thick file of clippings in the research library attests to the number of times over the past century that the street has been the subject of rehabilitation projects and guilds to restore its historical charm. These efforts have largely succeeded based on, if nothing else, the amount of pedestrian traffic it attracts on any given day.

There has been much debate among the local city officials about closing the street entirely to cars; at present, it is theoretically open to traffic but

Shelf array of miniatures.

technically shut down because of damage to the old buildings. A truck knocked the balcony off the nearby eighteenth-century Fatio-Ximenez house. It was the second time a truck has clipped an ancient colonial dwelling in two years.

It turns out that Aviles Street houses an array of structures of precious historical value, including the antique store. So, if Armstrong got the information about the building right, was he also right about the ghost? That, of course, is open to speculation. It's interesting that the ghost that "caught" the bulb was named Pedro, as in the Christian name of the Spanish founding father for whom the street is named. Was it a descendant? What is difficult to understand is how the relative of the admiral, confined to an old drunk tank, successfully played that on-the-run catch of the errant light bulb.

Antiques & Uniques Collectibles
7 Aviles Street
St. Augustine, Florida, 32084
https://www.facebook.com/pages/Antiques-Uniques-Collectibles

CASTILLO DE SAN MARCOS

Fortitude is the marshal of thought, the armor of the will, and the fort of reason.
—Francis Bacon

Some guidebooks refer to the Castillo de San Marcos as a rare and authentic national treasure. Other guidebooks refer to it as a castle. Its caretaker, the National Park Service, reveres its past—reenacting the Spanish-British conflicts, keeping up the grassy grounds and firing its cannons eternally pointed at Matanzas Bay. Tourists meander up and down the grassy Cubo and Rosario defense lines and press their ears to the ancient coquina walls, the walls that absorbed cannon shrapnel and sustained little damage from British cannon fire. There is the rumor that a strategic ear pressed against the thick walls will detect faint battle cries and muffled cannon fire. Castillo de San Marcos was, after all, a military outpost.

There are other paranormal stories as well. Prominent Indian prisoners languished in the fort's dungeons during the Seminole Wars, Chief Osceola among the most notable. Ghost tour guides describe an outline of the chief's visage appearing on the exterior face of the southern wall.

The Spanish left a psychic imprint as well. Supposedly, there is a lingering scent of perfume at the spot where a Spanish general walled his wife into a casement "Amontillado"-style, along with her lover. A headless soldier, from the first Spanish period, supposedly searches the terreplein for a lost wedding ring.

"Be careful what you say about the fort," Peter Gold, owner of St. Augustine Gold Tours, warns tourists. "They don't like to admit it's haunted, eh?"

Left: Exterior of Castillo de San Marcos.

Right: Re-creation of soldier's quarters.

What most people, the ghost tours and perhaps the National Park Service don't know is that human remains *have* been found inside the northeast corner of the fort. According to a nineteenth-century account written by Charleston volunteer Myer M. Cohen: "[o]ne of its many subterranean dungeons, not previously known, was discovered, and opened, when many human skeletons were found. The remains of the unfortunate tenants of these vaults were seen by the volunteers during our thirty days sojourn in St. Augustine." There was also a torture chamber, as well as an "oubliette," or a hole in the corner, "which… extended into quicksand and was used for the disposal of the dead," according to a 1930s text, *Souvenir of St. Augustine Under Three Flags: Pictorial History of Fort Marion.*

It would be quite a surprise for the sunburned family of five, out for a day of touring the ancient city, to stumble into these catacombs while looking for a place to deposit their chewing gum and see…what? A battalion of long-dead Spanish soldiers avenging the modern invasion of their fortress? Perhaps even the National Park Service can get behind that ghost story.

THEN AND NOW

According to an article in the 1937 restoration edition of the *St. Augustine Record*, "History of Ancient Coquina Fort Is Traced Through the Centuries," England's rousting of the Spanish Armada was such a humiliating debacle that it led to the calculated idea of the great fort. As early as 1595, the king of Spain received applications for a plan featuring "a stone fort" in St. Augustine.

Although Spain did not begin to build the Castillo de San Marcos until almost a century later, by that time rivalry with England over a stake in the New World had only intensified. In particular, Spain realized that St. Augustine's coastal fortifications, whose outposts included the Matanzas Inlet, the St. Marks River and the St. Johns River, consisted of only nine wooden forts and were inadequate to stem attacks from pirates. More importantly, the English naval ships were constantly vying to roust Spain from the hotly contested coastline.

So, in 1672, the Spanish began construction on the fort overlooking Matanzas Bay that was sequentially named Castle San Marcos, Fort St. Marks, Castillo de San Marcos, Fort Marion and, again, Castillo de San Marcos. Actually, according to historical text by Jane Landers, the Spanish settlers "had a disdain for manual labor," so Indians, slaves and free blacks from Fort Mose did all the hard work. Because of the humid, rainy weather and the toil involved in transporting construction materials, it wasn't completed until 1695, which was a rare accomplishment in itself, as few Florida forts were ever entirely finished.

Many unfinished Florida forts were made of brick. One reason for the success of Castillo de San Marcos was its composition. Constructed of coquina, a type of shell-rock quarried from nearby Anastasia Island, the use of available topographic resources was a clever construction strategy and no doubt contributed to its completion. Not that it was easy. Historical text divulges how laborers transported the coquina on barges and carried the blocks to the site on crossbars.

The fort was designed by Spanish engineer Ignacio Daza, whose plans revealed a "hollow square with four diamond-shaped bastions at each corner" (named after the apostles San Pedro, San Augustine, San Carlos and San Pablo), with "only one way in or out."

The fort grounds included a shot furnace, a powder magazine chamber, a chapel, prison cells, a central courtyard, guardrooms, a gun deck, storage rooms, a well, a moat (dry most of the time, as water compromised the fort's

Enclosed hollow
square of the
courtyard.

foundation), the Cubo-Rosario redoubts and the City Gates. Apart from prisoners, no one lived at the fort except during sieges when it was under attack. Then the St. Augustine townspeople, soldiers and the inhabitants of nearby Fort Mose streamed through the ravelin, a triangular fortification that protected the entrance, according to the National Park Service.

The ancient fort was attacked more than once. According to Alejandro Quesada, in his book *A History of Florida Forts*, three British invasions from the Carolinas, in 1702, 1728 and 1740 tested the coquina fortifications and its inhabitants. The coquina held up well under cannon fire, absorbing the shock of cannon shrapnel rather than shattering or crumbling as other materials did. The British were held off each time until 1763, when Spain gave St. Augustine to the British in return for retaining Cuba's Havana. It was the first of many territorial swaps in which the fort was the symbol of gain.

The British renamed the coquina fortress Fort Marion after a general, Francis Marion, who consequently, and ironically, became known as the "Swamp Fox" and the father of guerrilla warfare for the American rebels during the Revolutionary War. The fort bore his name, on and off, for decades.

Fort Marion was a prison for Indians during the Seminole Wars and was held briefly by the Confederates during the Civil War. The U.S. War Department owned it until the 1930s, when the National Park Service took over. In 1942, the fort regained its original name, the Castillo de San Marcos.

Today, the fort is an unmistakable focal point for the city of St. Augustine, similar to the Washington Monument in Washington, D.C. Since the masonry is the oldest in the continental United States, the fort is maintained under the care of the National Park Service and owned by the United States government, and thus it enjoys a federal tax exemption.

The fort today has restrooms, museum displays, a gift shop and colonial reenactments that include cannon fire. Picnickers use the grounds, and the Fourth of July festivities feature fireworks over the Matanzas Bay. In northeastern and central Florida, it is a rite of passage for fifth graders to travel by school bus to visit the great fort and then line up outside the City Gates to tour surrounding St. Augustine.

This brings us full circle to the issue of the fort's fate as a tourist destination. In a way, it was inevitable. The grounds cover more than twenty acres, and the fort stands more than thirty feet high at its tallest point. Its walls are between nine and twelve feet thick. Its behemoth bulk draws people, as it once drew refugees to stand within its fortressed walls. Yet there is another side to the Castillo de San Marcos that defies the happy picnickers lolling on its sloping grounds. It has been besieged, but it has never been seized.

Against the bright blue sky of St. Augustine, where it seldom rains, its decorative flags fluttering, the fort is nonetheless as gray and menacing and in-your-face as a medieval fortress, which is what it most closely resembles. This substantial slab, rising up out of its distinctive landscape, taunts time and stands apart from the collage of shops, tours and trivial distractions. We may learn details—what people ate, the weapons they used and how they dressed—but aside from the superficialities of a life that vanished long ago, the Castillo de San Marcos gives nothing up, especially its mystery. Only the ghosts retain its memories.

The Castillo de San Marcos
1 South Castillo Drive
St. Augustine, Florida, 32084
http://www.nps.gov/casa/index.htm

THE CARCABA FAMILY PLOT

He has got just what he has been looking for, I shot him.
—*Lottie Carcaba,* St. Augustine Record, *April 20, 1917*

Long before there was Casey Anthony, there was Charlotte Carcaba, a mercurial nymphet who seared a scandalous swath through the annals of Old St. Augustine society. Like Casey Anthony, she was young, attractive and selfish; she lied; and she was determined to have a good time no matter who or what got in her way, including her rich husband, her rich mother-in-law and her own children. She offered a ridiculous defense for her crime, and she made no apologies. There is one more similarity between her and the notorious Anthony narcissist: she got away with it.

According to the *St. Augustine Record*, Charlotte, aka "Lottie Falaney," was described as "the prettiest girl in St. Augustine" when she married the wealthy heir to a cigar factory, William H. Carcaba, in an "elaborate" ceremony in 1901. She was only fifteen years old, almost half the age of the well-established groom. A few years later, they started a family. There were two sons: first Eduardo and then, a year later, Hubert.

William's father was a prominent citizen and the founder of the first cigar factory in St. Augustine. Pantaleon Felix (P.F.) Carcaba, a man who briefly owned what is now the O.C. White's Seafood and Spirits Restaurant, was born in Havana and immigrated to Cincinnati, where he founded a successful cigar factory before settling in St. Augustine. According to accounts from the *St. Augustine Evening Record*, he was a shrewd businessman and a community

The brooding angel that guards the family.

leader so revered by the town that the mayor closed all the shops during his funeral so that everyone could attend.

William worked for him as a bookkeeper and, after his father's death, started up a new cigar factory on Ribaria Street with his brother-in-law, Augustin Solla. He and Lottie borrowed money from his mother, Barbara, to build a big house on San Marco Avenue. Life was good. William rated a mention now and then in the *St. Augustine Record* as a civic leader, a member of the Benevolent Order of Elks (P.F. Carcaba founded the local Elks Lodge) and as an all-around solid citizen.

Social prominence also extended to young Hubert Carcaba, according to a 1988 article in the *St. Augustine Record*. In 1912, as he stood on the corner of Mission Avenue, young Hubert saw a carriage stop. A portly man crossed the street and shook his hand. Hubert had just met Teddy Roosevelt.

The trouble started in 1916 when Lottie took a trip to North Carolina. When she came back, things were never the same. In October, she filed for divorce, charging William with "extreme cruelty," "a violent and ungovernable temper" and "habitual intemperance." William, fighting for custody of Eduardo and Hubert, declared that Lottie wouldn't let him see the children and "has given herself up to adulterous and licentious practices," according to the deposition record.

Incensed, Lottie filed a bill of complaint in November against Barbara, her mother-in-law, blaming her for the marital rift. According to the court document, Lottie said that Barbara "sought to prejudice the mind of William against her…to entice him to separate himself from the plaintiff, and to leave and desert her." Barbara, in her deposition, declared, "I have never at any time, since I have known Lottie shown any hostility towards her." She went on to say, "I have earnestly at all times tried to keep these two persons together as husband and wife."

It seems fair to say that in the early twentieth century in St. Augustine, the Carcabas, particularly Lottie, provided a distraction from looming national events, including a world war. Relations between the Carcabas continued to unravel at a dangerous pace. William moved out of the San Marco house, and Lottie stayed—that is, until she had to rent it out and move into a cottage in the back with the boys. She complained bitterly about money, claiming that William only gave her five dollars per week. According to case records, William countered, "My wife had no money until I married her." The last straw for William was when Lottie took up with the chauffeurs.

In April, America declared war on Germany, and William declared war on Lottie. Court files indicate that Victor White and Stephen Tompkins were strapping young men whom Lottie entertained at various times in her little cottage when the boys were away.

On the evening of April 20, 1917, while the boys were at the movies, William armed himself with a pistol and broke into the cottage. A shot was fired and then two more. A man in a white suit ran out of the house, jumped the fence and disappeared. Then William staggered out of the house, collapsed on the sidewalk and told the quickly gathering crowd, "I have been shot by Tompkins, the chauffeur, and I am dying." One police officer took off on a bicycle to chase down the suspect, and someone else flagged down a car to take William to the East Coast hospital. William died thirty minutes later. The entire incident was reported on the front page of the *St. Augustine Evening Record* with the headline, "W.H. Carcaba Was Shot and Killed Last Night."

Lottie defiantly declared that she had fired the fatal shot after her husband broke in through the back door and found her and the chauffeur alone in the darkened house. She claimed that William shot at her once, and she returned fire. According to eyewitnesses, the chauffeur ran away, and then a neighbor heard Lottie shout, "Get away from here; now go on, you have bothered me enough." She pushed William out of the door, where he staggered to the sidewalk and collapsed. Lottie was hauled off to the county jail, and William's brother took charge of Hubert and Eduardo.

William was buried on April 23 in the Carcaba family plot at Evergreen Cemetery parallel to his father's grave. According to the *St. Augustine Evening Record* in an article titled, "Laid to Rest," "great crowds thronged the street… and a large number followed the body to the cemetery to pay their last tribute to the deceased." The pallbearers were BPOEs (Benevolent and Protective Order of Elks).

It turned out that the chauffeur with Lottie that night was not Stephen Tompkins, as poor William suspected. Tompkins had an airtight alibi, and suspicion quickly settled on another chauffeur, Victor White. He was arrested, and an inquest was held the next day. He and Lottie Carcaba were indicted for first-degree murder in the circuit court of the Fourth Judicial Circuit of the State of Florida in and for St. Johns County. The trial for the two miscreants (*Florida v. Lottie Carcaba and Victor White*) began the next month, in May.

Lottie and Victor pleaded justifiable homicide and self-defense. Two .35-caliber pistols were found under a bedroom pillow. One gun was Lottie's, and one supposedly belonged to William. Her lawyer argued, "Gentlemen the right of a wife to claim self-defense when charged with shooting her husband is not changed or taken away by the fact that the husband at the time of the shooting had just discovered a man in his wife's dwelling house. The deceased broke into the dwelling house of defendant Lottie Carcaba with force and violence and with a pistol in his hand."

The trial lasted three weeks. The jury ruled that it "cannot convict either defendant unless you believe that Lottie and Victor at one and the same time pulled the trigger of the pistol." What really happened remained a mystery. Was the second gun really William's? If so, what was it doing under Lottie's pillow? Had Lottie and Victor ambushed him? How else had they managed such a clear shot in the dark? Regardless, Victor and Lottie were acquitted.

Lottie continued to live in the house on San Marco with her sons, but money was still tight. In December 1917, she took up her old lawsuit against her former mother-in-law, only this time she upped the damages to $100,000. Lottie said that she and William "lived happily together as husband and wife, and but for the wrongful and malicious acts of the defendant [Barbara]… would have continued to live together." The case was quickly dismissed, and Lottie received no money.

Lottie was back in court again in 1923, this time as the defendant. In 1915, William wrote a will leaving the house to the boys and a share to Lottie as long as she didn't remarry. Otherwise, it belonged to Hubert and Eduardo. Lottie hadn't remarried, but she wanted to sell the house. The suit brought against her was in the name of her eldest son, Eduardo, but it was filed by a family friend, Herman Manuey. Despite the legal claim of her sons, she won that round and sold the house for $14,000.

That is the last public record concerning Lottie Falaney Carcaba until her death notice in the *St. Augustine Evening Record* on the Ides of March in 1924. She died after an operation, and the newspaper identified her

The Carcaba family plot at Evergreen Cemetery.

formally as "Charlotte" and misspelled her maiden name. There was nothing personal about her in her obituary, yet it noted, "Her husband, the late William H. Carcaba, was for some years a prominent cigar manufacturer of this city." No businesses were closed in her honor, and there were no throngs of mourners in the street. Her brother, Wardy Falaney, held the funeral in the small dwelling she occupied on Nelmar Terrace, and she was buried without fanfare at San Lorenzo Cemetery. The San Marco house was torn down and today the site is the parking lot for the Shrine of Our Lady of La Leche.

Barbara survived her son and daughter-in-law and passed away on her birthday at the age of seventy-five in 1928. She was buried next to her husband, Pantaleon Felix. Augustin Solla, her son-in-law and William's business partner, was already there. Years later, Lula Solla, the Carcaba daughter and Augustin's wife, was buried next to her husband. Many years later, Hubert and his wife, Hallie, were buried side by side in the same plot.

There is no ghost to this story, but there is a haunting. A legacy lingers after life, littered in archives, letters, newspapers, books and, finally, etched into stone. Four Carcaba graves and two Sollas in the family plot are two and two—husbands and wives. There is a barren plot next to William; his headstone stands alone. Yet his family surrounds him, and a brooding stone angel guards the Carcaba family plot in Evergreen Cemetery. Forever.

THEN AND NOW

There is not much in the newspaper archives about the eldest Carcaba son, Eduardo, except that he lived to be eighty-six years old and died almost a year to the day after his wife Kathleen passed away. They are buried under the same headstone in San Lorenzo Cemetery.

Hubert, on the other hand, was a prominent figure in St. Augustine society along with his wife, Hallie. Like his father and his grandfather, he was a member of the BPOE, and he served as president of the St. Augustine Historical Society. Hallie was president of the Garden Society for many years. They had a long and happy marriage, and they both lived into their nineties. An acquaintance of theirs said, "At Hallie and Hubert's, when they had people over, they never talked about how his father died. If they said anything, they said that there was an accident and that it was a terrible tragedy. No one knew the details."

There is no printed evidence that Hubert ever mentioned his mother, Lottie, even once, in his long and illustrious lifetime. Since her crime, and since her various civil cases, not one more word was printed about Lottie Falaney Carcaba until now.

In one hundred years, one can only hope that is true of Casey Anthony as well.

Carcaba Family Plot
Evergreen Cemetery
505 North Rodriguez Street
Straight into entrance, first left
St. Augustine, Florida, 32084

CASA MONICA HOTEL

Who has benefitted by my presence?
—*Abbie Brooks,* Diary of Abbie M. Brooks

A s a rule, the Ancient City has a boundless scope and an enthusiasm for paranormal activity—except when it doesn't. Spokespeople for the Castillo de San Marcos, the Oldest Schoolhouse, the Spanish Military Hospital, the Lightner Museum and Flagler College were reluctant to verify spectral folklore or, in some cases, downright denied it. And then there's the Casa Monica Hotel, where the employees cheerfully acknowledge ghostly lore but are vague on details. They seem to live by the old Hindu proverb: "What does a fish know about water in which it has lived all its life?" To revise: "What does a Casa Monica employee know about ghosts in the place where he has worked every day?" And the answer: "Not too much."

Manny Perry has tended the granite bar in the ornate watering hole of the Casa Monica Hotel for a year. "They say it's haunted," he says placidly. He stumbles over the old saw about a woman in white, searches his memory for something better and says, "There's one girl—I'm filling in for her today—she's been here twelve years, she knows the hotel very well. She told me that she was in the Sultan's Room, the furthest room in the back, and she heard her name being whispered and there was nobody there." Perry has never had an encounter. He advises consulting with the concierge.

The concierge, Joshua Rowe, is a giant of a man, close to seven feet tall and dressed all in black. Yet there's nothing ominous about him, and he obligingly makes time for questions in between his many duties; the hotel

Interior of the Sultan's Room.

is bustling with guests checking in on an October afternoon, which is still considered the slow season. He says, "There's always stories of noises, of a thumping, of someone opening or closing a door, over and over again over a guest room. The only problem is there's no one checked in above that room." Then he offers, "There's a painting where the eyes are following you. It's creepy." He chuckles.

On the third floor, the portrait of Abbie Brooks (aka Silvia Sunshine), a nineteenth-century former schoolteacher, author and historian, is one of five "feisty" women commissioned for a posthumous portrait in honor of her contributions to St. Augustine. It is an oil on linen portrait, portraying a hatted woman in a red gown framed amid the backdrop of the hotel's Moorish pillars. Although she is dead and buried at St. Augustine's Evergreen Cemetery, her hooded eyes do seem to follow passersby. The whispers, the thumping, the door slamming and the running up and down the halls all point to a frantic search that, although Rowe didn't mention it, may culminate on the anniversary of her death, a destitute affair that occurred on Christmas Day. Speaking speculatively, what secret is she seeking to absolve? And who is she looking for?

The woman, whose penname is emblazoned as a glowing orb on her portrait, had an illegitimate daughter whom she gave up for adoption and never saw again. Perhaps that is what keeps Abbie Brooks around.

THEN AND NOW

A tourist can't shake a stick at a flamboyant architectural structure in Florida without turning up the name of Henry Flagler. The Casa Monica Hotel is no exception, although someone else influenced its design. In 1887, Flagler sold the land to one of his partners, Franklin Smith, and allowed him the expense of erecting a new grand hotel. Smith modeled the hotel after the style of his own winter home, the Villa Zorayda. Yet Flagler took no chances when it came to disabling potential competition with his much grander establishment, the Hotel Ponce de Leon (now Flagler College).

The Casa Monica Hotel—made of poured concrete and crushed coquina, designed in the Moorish Revival style and named after the saintly mother of the city's saintly namesake—opened in 1888 with only three guests and little in the way of furnishings. According to hotel lore passed down to Concierge Rowe, an anticipated delivery of the hotel's furnishings by Flagler's famous Florida East Coast Railway mysteriously failed to occur. A few months later, Smith was forced to sell the property to Flagler, who promptly renamed the hotel after an obscure Spanish village. Known as the Hotel Cordova, it served mainly as a reserve hotel for the Alcazar (now the Lightner Museum); Flagler even constructed a bridge between the two hotels. Yet the dearth of wealthy guests during the Great Depression caused the Cordova to close in 1932, just like its catty-corner hotel sisters the Ponce and the Alcazar.

It stood empty until 1962, when it was transformed into the St. Johns County Courthouse. An ironic footnote, according to bartender Manny Perry, is that civil servants, facing long lines of errant motorists, once staffed the same spot where tourists now toast one another's health around the granite bar. A historical footnote, according to local historian David Nolan, is that police dogs were kept in the lobby during the 1960s civil rights demonstrations. For more than thirty years, residents associated the hotel, Flagler's ill-gotten gain, with municipal matters.

Then, in 1997, another collector came to St. Augustine seeking sanctuary for his beloved artifacts. This time, it was not homespun hobbies enthusiast Otto Lightner but rather the worldly Richard Kessler who bought hotels (he owns seven of them, including the Grand Bohemian in Orlando, Florida) in which to store his artwork. He also cultivated and paid artists to decorate the rechristened Casa Monica. These artists included Marianne Lerbs of the five feisty women portraits (of which Abbie Brooks is one) and Jean Claude Ray, a famous French impressionist. Also prominently featured are the works of artist Lauren Denillo, whose unique canvas cloisonné still lifes are displayed in all of the main dining rooms.

These dining rooms are renovated in a Moorish design and feature names like the Gold Room, the Sultan's Room and the Wine Room, designed for intimate or formal dining experiences. Kessler spared no expense with furnishings and, not being reliant on Henry Flagler for their delivery, experienced no snags, although their origin was distant and exotic. There are hand-painted columns and beams, hand-made Moroccan lights and chandeliers and replicas of seventeenth-century Austrian imperial chairs. There are full-length paintings, red walls, fountains, heavy drapes on ornate curtain rods and terrazzo floors.

"What I like about it," Concierge Rowe says, "is that you don't feel like you're in Florida anymore; you feel like you're in a little European town. I lived in Europe for years, Italy and the Turk Republic, and this place sure reminds me of it. The central location, the shops close by, the cobblestone streets, the pillars, the art gallery." The Kessler art collection adjoins the hotel and is open to the public.

Although the hotel is listed as a National Historic Building, there are modern accoutrements, including a European-style café, a heated pool, a fitness center and an exclusive beach club. There are 138 guestrooms and deluxe and signature suites. Many St. Augustine events, including weddings, are held in the city's only AAA Four Diamond hotel.

All of the Casa Monica Hotel employees mentioned that they were still in "the slow season," which lasts until November 19, when the famous annual city celebration of the "Night of Light" occurs. The Spanish tradition of lighting a white candle to celebrate the nativity has ballooned into one of the American Business Association's top North American events. Millions of white lights illuminate St. Augustine trees and buildings, while the city celebrates with a regatta, concerts, ice-skating, celebrities and a Christmas parade. This, the hotel employees point out, marks the beginning of their busy season.

Exterior of the Casa Monica Hotel, with its cobblestone path.

It's no wonder that they barely have time to acknowledge their ghosts. In fact, it is easy to forget that the grand hotel—outfitted with fine art, exotic furnishings, fine food and wine—is as much a part of historic St. Augustine as the abutting cobblestone streets that retain the footsteps of the living and the dead.

On the third floor of the Casa Monica Hotel, an oil portrait of a woman watches the guests who come and go with omnificent interest. She benefits all with her historic presence.

The Casa Monica Hotel
95 Cordova Street
St. Augustine, Florida, 32084
http://www.casamonica.com

THE CITY GATES OF ST. AUGUSTINE

Such are the Gates of Paradise.
—*William Blake,* The Gates of Paradise

S t. Johns County has many "women in white" tales. Ghostly women wearing wispy white shrouds, uniforms or gowns reputedly haunt many places in St. Johns County. A bride floats above the Tolomato Cemetery. A starchy white nurse stalks the Spanish Military Hospital. Catalina de Porras, the Spanish lady who haunts Harry's Seafood Bar and Grille, is reported to drift in and out of walls in a trailing white dress. Pedestrians point to one staring out of a window at the Casa Monica Hotel.

However, the apparitions of the women in white make sense. These are southern ghosts, and women wore white during the humid summer months, during which time they often succumbed to yellow fever, childbirth or malaise. In fact, the ghost story about the City Gates of St. Augustine features not a woman, but a teenage girl in a white nightgown.

From Peter Gold of St. Augustine Gold Tours:

> *Elizabeth stands between the City Gates, somewhere to the right-end gate if you look at it and to the center. The story goes: she was the gatekeeper's daughter. She is one of the first to die of yellow fever. Now, to actually get a headstone in the Huguenot Cemetery, you had to pay four dollars. Father takes her and buries her over at Anastasia Island because he doesn't have any money to put her here in town. Having taken her over there, she*

The City Gates at night, when a "woman in white" waves to motorists.

regularly comes back here at night, is seen at night, standing outside the gates in a white smock with her long hair. She holds up her hands and says, "Don't come in. You'll get yellow fever." And they ring the sheriff, the strangers in town, who see her there, and they ring the police and say, "There's a girl that's been abandoned at the city gates, it's two o'clock in the morning." And that's the sort of reports the police get.

The ghost of the teenage girl, Elizabeth, who died of yellow fever in the early nineteenth century, is documented in Cain and Jacoby's book *A Ghostly Experience: Tales of Saint Augustine Florida*, in Stavely's book *Ghosts and Gravestones in St. Augustine Florida* and in Jenkins's book *Florida's Ghostly Legends and Haunted Folklore; North Florida and St. Augustine*. All three sources corroborate an "apparition" standing between the City Gates, sometimes waving at passing cars. The best time to see her is at about two or three o'clock in the morning, which is presumably the hour Elizabeth collapsed and died, stranded forever, not at the pearly portals of heaven but at the coquina gates of earthly St. Augustine.

THEN AND NOW

The City Gates used to be old, wooden and connected to the Castillo de San Marcos. Built in 1756, the sturdier coquina gates, one of the only original defensive structures still standing well into the twenty-first century, signified an attempt by the Spanish to fortify the town against British invasions. According to a 2005 article in the *St. Augustine Record* by Peter Guinta, the gates are a historic part of Spanish Florida's old "Cubo line." The old Cubo line, composed of dirt and palm logs, was a Spanish defense constructed along a moat spanning the San Sebastian River to the Castillo de San Marcos. Spaniards built the defense to ensure that they could man soldiers on all sides of the city, firing away at the British, who were attempting to negotiate the moat and get inside. It worked for the most part. The British burned the town to the ground, but they never took the fort.

A Historic Buildings Survey depicted the gate columns, which joined the east and the west, were restored from the original construction several times, the last being in the 1960s. Made of plastered coquina masonry and granite, the two square towers of the gate stand more than twenty-four feet high and are topped with ornate, curved replicas of pomegranates. Attached to coquina walls and guarding the drawbridge of a moat, they were the only entrance into the dirt roads of the city.

Today, the gates function as a portal to the ancient city. Opening on the north edge of St. George Street, the gates unveil the center of Old Town. On the other side are the art dealers, restaurants, gardens, museums, statues, fountains, fudge and ice cream stores, bars and T-shirt and gift shops of St. George Street. A pleasant stroll, the street is usually bustling with tourists, who spill out onto the Plaza de la Constitution on the other end near the city hall.

Remains of the original gates and the entrance to St. George Street.

It is hard to believe that an almost two-hundred-year-old "teenager," out late every night, hosts this bustling thoroughfare. Yet the tale of Elizabeth in her nightclothes, with her warning of yellow fever, connects the tourists in the Aloha shirts and the safari pants to an ancient trail of history that began long before her ghostly sojourn or their pleasant reality.

St. Augustine City Gates
1 Orange Street
Saint Augustine, Florida, 32084

FLAGLER COLLEGE

Try to remember, and if you remember, then follow…
—*Tom Jones,* The Fantasticks

According to gossip and legend, and according to the stories of some Flagler College students, many ghosts haunt the former Hotel Ponce de Leon. These include Henry Flagler, his wife, his mistress, a mysterious lady in blue and a young boy. Henry Flagler, owner and proprietor of the former hotel, moodily strolls the corridors and appears in dorms at the feet of students' beds, and his face is grotesquely etched on a tiny tile to the left of the entrance's main doors. His ghostly wife, Ida Alice, stares pensively at a panel wall that used to bear a portrait of her husband. His suicidal mistress still dangles from a chandelier on the fourth floor of the girls' dormitory. The late lady in blue bumps into furniture, which apparently was arranged differently 115 years ago. The little boy harasses female students.

Not every one believes that the college is haunted. Most students claim that they have never seen anything. The security guard in the main entrance hall said that he worked at the college for more than a decade and that he'd never had a supernatural experience and, furthermore, didn't believe that the Henry Flagler tile was really a likeness of the former magnate or of anything in particular. A student staffing a snack bar said, "Some people have had experiences. We don't really talk about it." She did confirm, however, that school officials bar students from the fourth floor, where Flagler's mistress died. It's been locked up for five years, undergoing renovations.

Exterior of the college.

In the face of such denial, a tourist may conclude that perhaps the college isn't haunted after all, and the ghost stories were merely the fevered imaginings of various tour guides. One of the bartenders at Harry's Seafood Bar and Grille says, "I'm not really the type of person who believes in ghost stories, generally. But something happened to me my sophomore year." The young bartender is Alana Mason, graphic arts major and senior at Flagler College. She dries glasses as she talks:

> I was living on the first floor of Ponce Hall in the east wing. One night, my roommate was out. I was staying there alone, and I was almost asleep. Then I felt this extreme pressure on my chest. It felt like someone was almost pressing on it with two hands. It was really strange. I looked around the room and made sure I was really awake. I kept pinching myself and looking around. And all of a sudden, I felt breath on my neck, and in my ear I heard, "Come play with me." And it just kept whispering it over and over: "Come play with me. Come play with me."

Interior of the rotunda, where ghost sightings have occurred.

I'm not the kind of person to believe in ghost stories, and I had no idea what it was. I was like crying and scared. I ended up just lying there, and it was like continuous—it wouldn't stop. I was just like lying there rigid, really scared. And the next morning, I was telling my RA [resident advisor] about it, because I was really scared. And she said, "That's really weird. Right where your room is there was a little boy who was playing with a ball and it fell over the rotunda, and he went after it and he died." And, like, right after she said that, I had, like, goose bumps all over me.

According to Stavely's *Ghosts and Gravestones in St. Augustine*, other Flagler College students have seen Alana's ghost, a ten-year-old boy in knee pants who "plays in the hallways." Ben Seth, a bartender at the Casa Marina Hotel in Jacksonville Beach, had this story to tell about the same little boy who appeared one night to his girlfriend, a coed at Flagler College:

She said it was the weirdest thing. She woke up in the dorm, and there was like this face above her, this apparition, trying to kiss her. She went to a local historian, who said, "Oh, I know who that is. It's a little boy who died in this hotel, and he messes with the girls. You're going to find bruises on the inside of your thighs. He likes to pinch." And you know, she did get all these bruises on the inside of her thighs.

Then and Now

It's been Flagler College since 1968, but it still looks like a grand hotel, which is what Henry Flagler, cofounder of Standard Oil and partner to John D. Rockefeller, intended when he built the 450-room Hotel Ponce de Leon in 1895. At the time, the site was just a marsh in what is now downtown St. Augustine, a city whose restorative climate and popularity appealed primarily to elderly invalids.

Flagler filled the swamp with dredged dirt exported from the north side of town—exported, in fact, from Fort Mose, the site of the first free black community in the United States (see Fort Mose State Park). The Hotel Ponce de Leon was consequently erected, in all its magnificence, on the soil of freed slaves. Across the street was a county jail; Flagler convinced local officials to tear it down by promising to build a new one a mile north of town (see St. Augustine Old Jail). He replaced the jail with the Hotel Alcazar

Bronze statue of Henry Flagler at the entrance.

(the Lightner Museum today) and, perpendicular to its sister hotels, the Cordova (today the Casa Monica Hotel). Despite the Spanish Renaissance style of the buildings, they were the first large structures in the United States constructed from concrete. The Hotel Ponce de Leon was also one of the first electrically wired structures in the United States.

It was a bold move to abandon the reliable, if consumptive, tourists, yet Flagler envisioned a resort getaway for his rich industrialist friends, a sort of American Riviera. When the hotel failed to thrive, Flagler flamboyantly purchased what eventually became the Florida East Coast Railway (now U.S. 1) so his guests would have transportation to his swanky resort. The former hotel rooms, now dormitories, once hosted famed men such as Admiral George Dewey, John Jacob Astor, Gary Cooper and Presidents Grover Cleveland and Theodore Roosevelt.

Today, Henry still presides over the entrance in the form of a hollow bronze statue just outside the gates of the private four-year liberal arts college.

Located in the heart of St. Augustine, across the street from the Lightner Museum, the college bell tower plays nostalgic show tunes such as the Fantasticks' "Try to Remember," which passing strollers can hear up and down King Street. A medieval spiked ball and chain fence surrounds the grounds, which include twenty-five acres of campus and 100,000 square feet of "intricately designed historic space," according to the Flagler legacy website.

The intricacy can be overwhelming, and there is a story behind all of it. Inside the gates, an ornate fountain also serves as a sundial. There are four turtles directly underneath the fountain base representing the seasons; twelve ceramic frogs encircling the fountain depict the hours of the day as they spit water into a cool blue basin. Framing the fountain is the impressive Spanish Revival Renaissance structure, a National Register treasure, replete with African mosaic tile flooring, gold plating, carved woodwork, nineteenth-century murals and a dining hall with million-dollar Tiffany stained-glass windows.

A substantial amount of money has been spent restoring the campus, yet the tuition is surprisingly reasonable for most middle-class families, and the college offers financial aid. There is a meal plan, but the school is close to several delectable restaurants, and there are also many fast-food restaurants within driving distance.

Although St. Augustine is clearly not a college town, the 2,500 students who attend Flagler College are noticeably present, strolling through town and lounging around the grounds, studying, socializing and talking politely to their elders, which includes visiting parents and many tourists. They try to ignore the ghosts.

Flagler College
74 King Street
St. Augustine, Florida, 32084
http://www.flagler.edu

FORT MATANZAS NATIONAL PARK

Lord, remember all my afflictions, and me…
—*Jean Ribault,* The Whole & True Discoverye of Terra Florida

Since the national park is the site of the famous massacre of French Huguenots by Admiral Pedro Menéndez de Aviles, and since the name of the fort, and the river, is literally *Matanzas*, meaning "place of slaughter," one would expect ghost stories galore despite the inherent reticence of pragmatic park rangers to acknowledge otherworldly reenactments of history. However, there are no ghost stories of Jean Ribault, the French Protestant explorer who hoped "to build a house for the Lord" on Florida soil. Historical accounts reveal that poor Ribault was poked with a spike, and his head was hacked into four distinct pieces, yet no one has seen him or his men haunting the nature trail, shaking their translucent fists at startled tourists.

Instead, the ghosts of Fort Matanzas, if there are any, are more recent and less historic. In fact, they have a less than sterling reputation as squatters. According to Fort Matanzas park ranger Kevin McCarthy, this happened because President Jackson, during his tenure as governor of Florida, dumped the fort. He did it because the fort was small and old, and America owed more money in 1819, comparatively, than it owes today. So, Fort Matanzas sat unfunded and unencumbered in the inlet, some miles south of the much larger and more famous Castillo de San Marcos.

Yet the word "unencumbered" does not mean unoccupied. Ranger McCarthy said that real squatters actually lived in the fort until the late

1920s, when President Coolidge declared it a national monument. By then, the fort was a mess—the coquina walls were crumbling, the sentry box had fallen into the drink and the gun deck was a shambles. The National Park Service did not make much progress with repairs until the Great Depression in the 1930s, when the Works Progress Administration (WPA) took over and finally completed the restoration.

The only ghost story one can pry out of Ranger McCarthy has to do with three fishermen who stayed at the fort in the 1930s. In the guardroom, they built a fire on the old hearth. Lightning struck the fort, traveled down the chimney and electrocuted the three men as they sat there with their hands outstretched to the fire, some freshly caught fish, no doubt, laid aside for their meal. Apparently, there have been sightings of the unfortunate trio.

So, according to current lore, sixteenth-century French soldiers caught up in a religious and territorial crusade, ending in their bloody massacre, do not haunt the fort. Instead, the ghosts of Fort Matanzas are American men driven by desperate economic circumstances to seek shelter in a crumbling stone fort where they were struck by a bolt of lightning.

It just goes to show that even ghost stories of haunted places evolve to become socially relevant.

THEN AND NOW

Fort Matanzas National Park is right across the street from Crescent Beach on A1A in St. Johns County, about fifteen miles south of St. Augustine. A family of great horned owls (literal snowbirds) roosts every winter in an old squirrel's nest, high in a cedar tree, and raise one or two owlets that fledge in the spring. There is a pontoon boat ride out to the old coquina fort on Rattlesnake Island (a barrier island), where tourists walk the dirt floor of the ammo room, observe the four bunks in the guard's room (slightly elevated at the heads, with rough blankets folded at the feet) and climb the narrow ladder to the observation deck, where the Spanish flag still flies. Salt marshes stretch out by the fort, and there are wild oyster beds framing the inlet and good fishing to be had.

Now on the National Register of Historic Places, the fort wasn't even built in 1565, when Ribault unwisely set out by ship from nearby Fort Caroline, a French settlement, to fight the Spaniards for possession of St. Augustine. Since Spain had already claimed Florida, King Philip was enraged by the

French fort, an illegal arrangement as far as he was concerned. So, a huge showdown was scheduled between the Spanish Catholic Menéndez and the French Huguenot Ribault.

Ribault predicted victory and then sailed directly into an August hurricane. The surviving soldiers were shipwrecked and made their way slowly back toward Fort Caroline—just imagine how hot it was in those heavy wet clothes. Local Indians pointed them out to Menéndez, who picked them off in small straggling groups. He and his men captured the Huguenots, made them surrender, took them behind the sand dunes and then offered to free them if they'd convert to Catholicism. Most of them, including Ribault, refused. So the Spaniards stabbed them with rough wooden bayonets and then rounded up the next batch until 275 of the Huguenots were dead. Then they went on to kill all the men, women and children at Fort Caroline. Small wonder that that the register of park visitors by the gift shop contains the snarky entry, "vive le France."

At any rate, tourists can see the approximate spot of the Huguenot massacre from the nature trail. There's actually a stone marker, which notes, all in caps, "MASSACRE BY MENÉNDEZ OF RIBAULT AND HIS MEN, SEPTEMBER 1565." Then there's another, more gruesome marker with a drawing of the massacre occurring.

Aside from its bloody history, the park is home to many rare and common birds, insects and wildlife. The park even issues a list of species. It is family friendly; a Channel 13 news crew has filmed the park for its series *Florida on a Tankful*. A half-mile nature walk, dappled by sunlight, is visible through a twisted canopy of live oaks. There is always a line of tourists waiting to board the pontoon boat for the fifty-minute Fort Matanzas tour, their kids playing on the beach while waiting.

From a distance, the fort looks as if a fourth-grader constructed it out of Legos. It is so small that four Fort Matanzases could fit in the courtyard of the Castillo de San Marcos. Yet the initial design was never grand; the whole idea of Fort Matanzas began as a series of wooden watchtowers in 1569. The Spaniards built the actual fort on the barrier island in 1742 out of coquina bricks and a tabby (oyster shell) mixture. Fort Matanzas, which only held about seven officers, was meant to reinforce the Castillo de San Marcos by guarding the rear of St. Augustine from pirates and approaching vessels. This strategy did not work so well with the wooden watchtowers when Sir Francis Drake sacked St. Augustine in 1586, but it did better from the stone fort when Governor General Oglethorpe attacked in 1742. In fact, because of the efforts of Fort Matanzas and Fort Mose, Oglethorpe never attacked again.

Left: Site of the Huguenot massacre of Ribault and his crew of 275 men.

Below: Exterior of Fort Matanzas.

Tourists can hear the not-so-rapid-fire weapon systems demonstration performed by the Fort Matanzas reenactors dressed in their red and white knickers, breeches and three-cornered hats. A visitors' center plays a video history of the three hundred acres that compose the park on continuous loop. A little boy in a junior ranger hat runs up to his mother, with a small coin in his hand. "Look at this," he says. "This is treasure."

Beyond the coquina gift shop, the inlet glitters where the Spanish king's fleets, laden with pricey cargo, once searched for the straits of the Gulf Stream. Yet there is both tangible and intangible treasure. Fort Matanzas was built to protect the former, and it endures to protect the latter.

Fort Matanzas National Park
8635 A1A South
St. Augustine, Florida, 32080
http://www.nps.gov/foma/index.htm

FORT MOSE STATE PARK

We have come, treading our path through the blood of the slaughtered /
Out from the gloomy past...
—*James Weldon Johnson*, Lift Every Voice and Sing

There are no ghosts at Fort Mose State Park, but it is haunted nevertheless. Located about two miles north of St. Augustine, the dry land where the forts stood almost three centuries ago is now an island of grass on a brackish marsh. A forest of live oak, red bay and holly predominate the eastern divide of the state park, and red cedar proliferates along the western end. It is quiet, brooding and deserted. Near sundown, no one hears the lonely hoot of an owl.

Missing is the cardboard placard proclaiming when and where the local paranormal tour begins. The chattering ghost tours of St. Augustine—with their entourage of camera-carrying, orb-seeking tourists—are noticeably absent. Yet there is a distinct spiritual sense to the state park commemorating the first free black community in the United States.

Bernadette "Miss B" Reeves, a local actress and storyteller, was quoted in a 2007 *Jacksonville Times-Union* article by Terry Brown, "First Road to Freedom," as saying, "I find when I walk the grounds of Fort Mose and run my hand over the bushes, the spirits of my ancestors call out to me, thanking me for continuing to tell their story."

Despite its lack of paranormal attention, if there is one place in St. Johns County where spirits would be expected to "call out," it is Fort Mose State Park. It is the site of a famous eighteenth-century battle (with a Spanish

Landscape where Fort Mose once stood.

victory) known as "Bloody Mose." It is a battle that rousted and disheartened the English forces of Georgia governor James Oglethorpe.

Its heroes were a black and Indian militia composed primarily of freed African slaves. A former slave, the brave and dashing Captain Francisco Menendez, led them. They killed seventy-five English invaders in hand-to-hand combat and, for good measure, castrated and beheaded the wounded. According to a letter St. Augustine governor Don Manuel de Montiano wrote to the Spanish sovereign regarding the English commander of Bloody Mose, "an Indian prisoner affirms positively that he saw Col. Palmer dead and his head cut off."

Who haunts Fort Mose State Park? Is it Oglethorpe's headless English invaders? Is it Menendez's soldiers? The valiant veterans of the former black settlement relocated to Cuba along with the Spanish in 1763 when the first Spanish period ended. History tells us that they never returned to the blood-soaked site of their former village.

History also tells us that what is past belongs to us forever. The echoes of Fort Mose persist even though the voices are from the past. You can hear it at sundown. You can hear it when you are quiet.

THEN AND NOW

American slaves actually went *south* seeking freedom one hundred years before the Emancipation Proclamation or the establishment of the famous Underground Railroad. Primarily from South Carolina rice plantations, southern slaves enlisted the help of friendly Indians to make their way to "Spanish Florida" and the black settlement of Fort Mose, north of St. Augustine. In 1693, King Charles II of Spain issued an invitation to American slaves, saying that if they could make it to St. Augustine, if they pledged allegiance to the Spanish Crown and if they converted to Catholicism, they could stay as free men and women. In 1733, he formalized his offer as a royal edict.

Spain had always had a more benign approach to slavery than its English and American counterparts. Spaniards gave their slaves the opportunity to earn their freedom, observe the sacraments of marriage and, as a rule, keep their families together. This approach worked for everyone in Spanish Florida. For the Spanish, Fort Mose citizens provided invaluable manual labor sorely needed to clear land, plant crops and construct forts. In fact, the first laborers on the famous Castillo de San Marcos were freed slaves. In addition, the men and women of Fort Mose brought their skills as artisans, masons, ironworkers, trappers, fishermen and farmers. For them, taking advantage of Spanish-English animosity was a way to win their freedom and consequent sanctuary in Florida. The fort itself, built in 1738, provided an important northern line of defense for the town of St. Augustine.

Fort Mose was small, less than one-fourth of an acre and made of stone, dirt and logs. It was of simple construction with a well, a watchtower and a dry moat bordered with cactus. Outside the fort were the resident houses, mostly simple thatched structures. During an attack, the people of Fort Mose could retreat to their own fort or, as they did in the case of Oglethorpe's invasion, flee to the Castillo de San Marcos.

During the 1742 repulsion of the British, Fort Mose burned down. The former residents moved to the city of St. Augustine and lived among the townspeople for twelve years, forming strong family bonds with one another, freed slaves, slaves, Indians and even some of the white residents, as interracial relationships were common. Then, a new governor replaced the benign Montiano. The freed slaves were removed from St. Augustine, and a new Fort Mose was built. It was bigger than the first one but essentially occupied the same grounds. About sixty-seven men, women and children lived there self-sufficiently.

Things changed in 1763 when the Spanish Crown handed St. Augustine over to the British. The British had a much harsher practice of slavery than the Spaniards and most assuredly would not have honored the free status of the men and women of Fort Mose. These brave citizens faced almost certain enslavement from which there was no recourse. They had no choice but to opt for evacuation to Cuba, which they did along with the Spaniards. Many Spaniards returned to St. Augustine in 1784 for the second Spanish period, even reclaiming their homes. None of the Fort Mose settlers did, not even

Captain Francisco Menendez, who commandeered the Fort Mose militia for forty years. He moved to Havana and reportedly died there.

Today, some people, such as local historian and Fort Mose reenactor James Bullock, keep the memory of the settlement alive. Bullock has written a play about the African American community titled *Freedom Road* that is performed in local venues. In addition, the National Park Service honored Fort Mose in 2009 as the forerunner to the National Underground Railroad Network to Freedom.

Yet nothing of either of the two Fort Moses remains. Natural elements are responsible, such as rain, wind, heat and erosion. Development interests also altered the geographic terrain; in the 1880s, oil magnate Henry Flagler dredged land from Fort Mose to use as fill for two of his three hotels in downtown St. Augustine.

Still, tourists can see the site where the settlement once stood. In 1988, the State of Florida began to take steps to acquire the land and, in 1994, succeeded in making Fort Mose a state park and a national historic landmark. The Fort Mose website features a picture of former governor Jeb Bush and local residents shoveling dirt at the groundbreaking ceremony.

The state park is about forty-two acres, containing a museum, a visitors' center, a nature trail, an interpretive exhibit, picnic and restroom facilities and self-guided tours. The park is a bird habitat to rare species such as the wood stork, the great blue heron and the gray catbird. At one time, prior to the 2004 hurricanes, there was even a bald eagle nest.

A long boardwalk opens onto a saltwater marsh where the forts actually stood. All that remains of Fort Mose is underground now, the home of snakes, rabbits, turtles and hermit crabs. There is a skyline of apartment buildings to the south, and there are houses on the other side of the river. It does not seem like much, especially compared to the pace and the vigor of more compelling attractions.

Yet if Fort Mose teaches us anything, it is that there is a story *behind* everything, even a flat piece of earth. The story of Fort Mose, like its erratic and interrupted history, has been lost and found and trickled through the forgotten undercurrents of history. Every time it is discovered, it emerges from the gloom of the past.

Fort Mose State Park
15 Saratoga Boulevard
St. Augustine, Florida, 32084
http://www.floridastateparks.org/fortmose

HARRY'S SEAFOOD
BAR AND GRILLE

*The foolish and wicked practice of profane cursing and swearing is a vice so
mean and low that every person of sense and character detests and despises it.*
—*George Washington, "Washington's Order Against Profanity"*

Erica Andrew, a bartender at Harry's Seafood Bar and Grille, has a ghost
story about Catalina de Porras, the Spanish eighteenth-century former
mistress of the current New Orleans–style restaurant on Avenida Menéndez.
Erica works the bar on the second floor (accessible by a steep stairwell),
which has an overflow dining hall with a great view of the bay. Around the
corner is the ladies' restroom that Catalina reportedly haunts. Not content
to appear in the mirrors while female patrons powder their noses, Catalina
also makes her presence known in the restaurant on special occasions. Here
is Erica's story:

> *Late at night, I was here at the bar. A ghost tour came through. All the ghost
> tours, they come in here. And there was a gentleman, and he was, like, every
> other word out of his mouth was a cuss word. Every other word. The tour
> guide warned him—she always stresses when she come in here, "Be careful
> when you curse at Harry's, Catalina doesn't like it. Be careful. Strange things
> happen when you curse." And it was so weird, I was standing right there,
> and all of a sudden, his head flew back, and he had a bloody nose. Out of
> nowhere. So, it was just, strange, it was really weird. We said, "I told you."*

Erica also says that a swarm of flies has pestered particular patrons. According to Jenkins's *Florida's Ghostly Legends and Haunted Folklore*, paranormal activities at Harry's range from odd noises to scents to ghostly visions in mirrors or to a glimpse of a woman from the corner of an eye.

The infamous restroom, which is supposed to be in the same spot as Catalina's former bedroom, is quaint, with two bathroom stalls, a vanity and a shuttered window with a dumpster directly below. Tourists prepare to leap through the window if Catalina materializes and, in the interest of research, often curse, low and under their breath. Usually nothing happens. One wonders how long and how late one has to sit at the bar in order to rile her. Apparently, in life and in death, Catalina is not prepared to compromise in any way.

THEN AND NOW

Catalina de Porras, of 46 Aviles Menéndez Street of St. Augustine, appears to have been a woman of a singular and stubborn disposition. Born in 1753, she was only ten years old at the end of the second Spanish period, when she and her family were displaced to Cuba along with the rest of Spaniards and the freed slaves of nearby Fort Mose. Her mother had an eight-week-old infant, and the resettlement was hard on everyone. However, in 1784, at the beginning of the second Spanish period, "Catalina de Porras was able to reclaim the St. Augustine house her mother received as a dowry many years earlier," according to Jane Landers as reported in her tract "The Floridanos in Cuba."

She was married by then, but she brought her husband, Joseph Xavier Ponce de Leon, whose parents were also natives of St. Augustine. The Spanish couple dug in to the process of reclaiming the mansion, which had been used as a storehouse for the British military for two decades. It took Catalina five years to work through the deed. Then she moved the cannonballs out, and she and her husband moved in about 1789. They had a daughter, Manuela Ponce de Leon.

Catalina died a few years later. Her daughter sold the house and moved back to Cuba in 1821. Although Yahoo Travel touts Harry's Seafood Bar and Grille as "one of the oldest houses in St. Augustine, built in 1740," the original De Porras house burned down in 1887. It served as a boardinghouse and four successive restaurants: the Puerta Verde, the Chart House, Catalina's Gardens and Harry's.

Exterior of the reconstructed former home of Catalina de Porras.

Today, the only original part of Harry's is the garden wall; it survived because it is made of poured concrete. Still, the current house is modeled after the same general configuration as the original De Porras mansion, which was rebuilt based on sketches of the original. There are Victorian details, such as boxcar siding, a wooden staircase and ornate mantelpieces. There are two entrances of arched stone—one from Charlotte Street, the back entrance, and one from Aviles Menéndez, the front entrance. Both open into an outdoor atrium, an attractive dining area, where it is not easy to get a table amid the potted palm trees strung with sparkling white lights.

If you want to see Catalina, go late at night, hang out at the upstairs bar and take a trip to the powder room. Watch your language, though. For a ghost, Catalina packs a mean punch.

Harry's Seafood Bar and Grille
46 Avenida Menéndez
St. Augustine, Florida, 32084
https://hookedonharrys.com/locations/st-augustine

HUGUENOT CEMETERY

Never trust the teller, trust the tale.
—*D.H. Lawrence,* Women in Love

Accounts vary among ghost tour tellers as to whether the Huguenot Cemetery is *really* haunted. They say it's haunted, of course, but the extent to which spirits flock to the half-acre just outside the City Gates is debatable. Charles Carlson wrote in *Weird Florida*, "The Huguenot Cemetery is the most haunted cemetery in the Ancient city; you might say it is 'Spirit Central.'" John Stavely stated in *Ghosts and Gravestones in St. Augustine Florida*, "Many sightings take place at this accessible location."

Not so, according to Peter Gold, a licensed walking and tour guide, who tools tourists through the ancient streets in his St. Augustine Gold Tours bus. A former barrister from Manchester, England, Gold says that the cemetery is "not very much haunted." He contends that artificial borders confine the sanctioned space. "All the bodies are buried outside," he says flatly. "Bodies are buried everywhere. Inside and outside the gates."

His point, which he reiterates often, is that a cemetery is small potatoes, a microcosm of psychic activity when it comes to St. Augustine. Cemetery gates are far too confining for spirits. "This whole town is haunted," Gold says.

His hypothesis does more to explain the limitless convergence of paranormal business activity in Florida's oldest city than the actual presence of ghosts. However, there are many Huguenot Cemetery ghost stories. There is that tired old saw about Judge Stickney, whose ten-foot marble monument belies the fact that he's not even buried at the Huguenot Cemetery; he was exhumed and transported to Washington, D.C., at the request of his children. Gold's version of the oft-documented tale about Stickney's ghost roaming the cemetery searching for his gold teeth, which grave robbers stole during his exhumation, offers nothing new.

The cemetery gates are locked, so no one can actually enter the graveyard, especially vandals, which is the point. Gold often leads tourists to the iron gates at the rear of the cemetery. "There are three graves of young men around here. All died in the same month of January 1835. According to local lore, they like to party with the girls. Put your hand through the gate," Gold tells the ladies. "You'll get yanked."

Gold is actually on to something here. According to the New England Historical and Genealogical Register concerning "Inscriptions in the Old Protestant Graveyard in St. Augustine, Florida," three young men

Three spooky graves.

hailing from New York and Massachusetts, and ranging in age from twenty-three to thirty-five years of age, bear identical upright headstones inscribing their death in January 1835. They are Erastus Nye, John Hull and John Lyman.

Karen G. Harvey, a St. Augustine historian who helped develop one of the first St. Augustine ghost tours, wrote in her book *Oldest Ghosts*, "We… know they are restless spirits…one attractive young woman confessed to something 'grabbed' her leg." Supposedly, Nye, Hull and Lyman like to trip people, tip hats and tap people on the shoulder—particularly if they're young, attractive and female.

"I bring all the girls here," Gold says. "One night, Erastus pinched a girl's bottom."

Gold says something else intriguing. "This cemetery was supposed to be for Protestants who died of yellow fever. Well, there are precious few headstones for 1821 when they all died."

As it turns out, he's dead right.

THEN AND NOW

According to the historical marker, certified with the Great Seal of Florida, the Public Burying Ground, off State Road A1A, was founded during the yellow fever epidemic of 1821, coinciding with the year that the United States took over occupation of the formerly Spanish territory. Since the Tolomato Cemetery on Cordova Street didn't bury non-Catholics, the city fathers received permission from the government to use the land, previously owned by Spain, for a public cemetery. In 1832, the land was deeded to the Presbyterian Church, which still owns and maintains the cemetery. It is known as the Huguenot Cemetery, although there are no actual Huguenots (French Protestants) resting in the Public Burying Ground.

In 1821, St. Augustine, a new American territory, was rife with tourists, as it is today. In fact, many were invalids or typhoid victims hoping to restore their health in the balmy climate. Many others were young men, making a new life. But the confusion over the Spanish departure left the city in a condition of dirt and disrepair. Worse, a yellow fever epidemic soon brought the disease raging into the St. Augustine harbor, where ships went back and forth from Florida to Havana, with no effort to isolate sick passengers or crew.

There is no doubt that the 1821 yellow fever epidemic decimated the city of St. Augustine. The church ceased the tradition of ringing the church bell when someone died; otherwise, it rang constantly. Residents and tourists died in droves.

Historic lore places nineteenth-century non-Catholic yellow fever victims within the borders of the half-acre cemetery. Yet a study of the inscribed stones turns up only three graves attributed to the year 1821, when yellow fever raged. These are I.G. Happoldt, fifty-three years old; Samuel Fleischman, fourteen years old; and William R. Whilden, four years old. The majority of existing headstones mark the dates of death from 1835 until 1884, when the cemetery closed and interments moved farther out of town.

There are several explanations for the lack of physical documentation of the demise of St. Augustine's population to yellow fever. Wooden grave markers rotted away. Some bereaved families couldn't afford a headstone, and it was common for nonwhite citizens to be buried without markers. Then there was the issue of the cemetery's upkeep.

Today, the Presbyterian Friends of the Huguenot Cemetery scrupulously maintains the graveyard. In the 1820s, the grounds were in disarray. At one time, there wasn't even a fence to section off the site. Ralph Waldo Emerson, visiting in 1827, wrote in his journal, "There are two graveyards in St. Augustine, one of the Catholics, another of the

Unique coquina crosses.

Protestants. Of the latter, the whole fence is gone, having been purloined by these idle people for firewood."

It is logical, then, to surmise that many yellow fever victims were anonymously buried whenever and wherever, outside and around the gates of the actual cemetery. Although the history of the careless upkeep of the cemetery boundaries may give some tourists pause as they stroll the exterior grounds, the Huguenot Cemetery is quite beautiful, and it is historically and architecturally significant. Charles Bulow, the sugar plantation magnate, is buried here, as is Eliza Whitehurst, a businesswoman and manager of an inn built in the eighteenth century (now the Ximenez-Fazio House Museum).

The best pictures are taken from the west side of the cemetery, where the wall of the Castillo de San Marcos provides a backdrop. Spanish moss drips from century-old trees, overhanging the ornate grave markers. The grave sites are charmingly and irregularly placed. Many are fenced off and composed of different kinds of materials: marble, stone and even coquina. In fact, there are two coquina crosses in the cemetery, unique because coquina is seldom carved into shapes given its crumbly shell texture. These two coquina crosses in the Huguenot Cemetery may be the only ones of their kind in the entire world. Clearly, the cemetery conveys a distinct historical authenticity to the city of St. Augustine, despite the antics of its irreverent spirits.

Huguenot Cemetery
Off A1A across from the City Gates
Closed to the public

THE LIGHTNER MUSEUM

I alone and the midnight star, keep watch in the court of the Alcazar.
—anonymous

Chris Koons, who often operates the entrance to the Lightner Museum, makes a wry face when a tourist asks for a ghost story about the former Hotel Alcazar. "There are no ghost stories," she says. "I ought to know. I've been here fourteen years."

"Doesn't the ghost tour stop here?" the man asks.

Ms. Koons laughs. "They [the ghost hunters] never let the truth get in the way of a good story." But what if the ghost story is about the ghost tour? Here's the good ghost story about the ghost tour to the Lightner Museum, told by local café proprietor Diane Ladd:

> *Two ladies who missed the tour went to the Lightner Museum one night to take pictures. Two ladies from Germany. They said they went to the gate, and of course, it's closed. They saw a gentleman at the gate, and they were trying to talk to him to get him to open the gate or to ask him questions. They said he looked at them a couple of times, and then he just walked away. And they came back the next day and they were talking about how rude he was. Well, they went on a tour of the Lightner museum, and they saw his picture. On the wall. Well, it was O.C. Lightner that they claimed to have seen. So, I guess he really wasn't being rude [chuckle]. He was just heading back into wherever it was he was going to. But they swear that's who it was that they saw.*

Did the German tourists see a ghost? Was it the famous proprietor of the museum still overseeing his beloved collectibles? There's a reason the story is interesting, and the reason has to do with information that most people don't know about Otto Curtis Lightner. He's buried in the courtyard of the Lightner Museum.

Then and Now

The Hotel Alcazar was the second of Henry Flagler's grand hotels, the first being the Hotel Ponce de Leon (now Flagler College), which stood directly across the street. Both were made of poured concrete and built on soil dredged from the creek bed on the northern end of town—from Fort Mose, the first free black settlement in Florida. *Alcazar* means "castle" or "palace" in Arabic, and like the Ponce, it was intended to appeal to Flagler's friends, all wealthy northern tourists of the late nineteenth century.

The Hotel Alcazar differentiated itself from the Hotel Ponce de Leon because of its recreational facilities, including a two-lane bowling alley, tennis courts, a casino and a movie theater. It had three floors and the world's largest indoor swimming pool, 120 feet by 50 feet, fed from an underground spring. The

Gated entrance to the Lightner Museum.

The garden leading to the bridge.

Exterior of the Lightner Museum.

second floor had an avant-garde spa with a massage parlor, a sauna, a steam room, sulfur baths and a gymnasium. The third floor was a ballroom, where guests and locals held parties.

Townspeople used the hotel to swim or to bowl. Thomas Edison liked to stay there, and humorists such as Will Rogers entertained in the casino. Then, like the Ponce, it closed during the Depression in 1931, when all of Flagler's wealthy friends lost their loot in the stock market crash. The Hotel Alcazar stood vacant until 1946.

Then the Chicago publisher of *Hobbies* magazine, Otto C. Lightner, bought the Alcazar. A self-made man who started out as a typesetter, Lightner became a rich man in a position to buy such things. He wanted to bring his Gilded Age (a period in American history after the Civil War up to the stock market crash) collections to Florida. Lightner accumulated his collection from items he bought from estate sales of former millionaires who lost everything during the Depression. He collected collections—furnished rooms and even entire houses. And he needed somewhere to put his artifacts.

He was staying at the Ponce when he looked across the street and saw what would later be promoted as the "Smithsonian of the South." It was just a grand shell, devoid of commerce or purpose yet far too beautiful to serve as a warehouse. It was perfect for Lightner's purposes. So he bought it for $125,000; the building alone is worth more than $7 million today.

Lightner transported his collection from Chicago to Florida in trucks, suffering expense and theft along the way. The museum opened two years later, in 1948. According to a 1949 editorial in the *St. Augustine Illustrated Sun*, the city fathers didn't appreciate it. The editorial, which includes comments from disgruntled taxpayers, berates Mr. Lightner for creating a tax-free "historic shrine." St. Augustine citizens wanted the lavish hotels stocked with the freewheeling spenders to return. Instead, they got a folksy Chicago publisher who wrote prosy and practical op-ed, articles and essays about crops and economics.

Otto Lightner was a man who encouraged everyone to cultivate hobbies and spend their money on collecting items that would appreciate in aesthetic value. Oh, how the city missed Henry Morrison Flagler, with his mistresses, his flair and his greenbacks, fluttering out of his silken waistcoats. Instead, they were stuck with a midwestern rube who paid no taxes and offered no revenue or recreation other than his geeky collectibles, which he, bearing no grudges, left to the city when he died.

The Lightner Museum, like Flagler College, boasts a Spanish Renaissance Revival style and is listed on the National Register of Historic Places. It stands in a courtyard with Lightner's headstone and a bridge arching over a fishpond. The lobby retains the look of the Hotel Alcazar: terrazzo floors, pillars, statues and crystal chandeliers. The vast swimming pool is now an antique mall with a café, but the ballroom, like the lobby, was restored to its original ornate splendor.

There is a nominal fee to enter the Lightner Museum (discounted for local residents) where visitors give up their bags and parcels and then take a quick jaunt through the Lightner Museum Store, which sells books, jewelry, ornaments, cards and faux antiques, games and gifts. There are three rooms at the first level, and an elevator in the science room takes visitors upstairs. Cameras are allowed.

The Lightner Museum has attempted to represent themes in its displays, but much of what is represented on the three floors is eclectic, which adds to its charm. There is a huge display of cut, Depression-era and Tiffany glass. There is also furniture, sculpture, paintings, curios, artifacts, clothing, musical instruments and a mummy. The Café Alcazar, located near the antique mall, offers lunch. The Junior Service League hosts an annual gala in the mall.

Visitors hoping for relics of old St. Augustine will be disappointed, but there are other venues available for such viewings (such as the Visitor Information Center at Fort Mose State Park). The Lightner Museum displays only the taste, enthusiasm and largess of its benevolent collector, who donated a beloved hobby to generations of St. Augustinians and its tourists.

Unlike the bold life-size bronze statue of Henry Flagler across the street in front of the college, only an unobtrusive eight- by eleven-inch portrait of O.C. Lightner hangs on the wall facing the entrance to the museum. The sound of his self-playing mechanical musical instruments provides a cacophonic backdrop. Information about his private life is hard to find. But what about his afterlife? Perhaps he really, as the German tourists avow, still walks the grounds of the museum, overseeing his collection.

The Lightner Museum
75 King Street
St. Augustine, Florida, 32084
http://www.lightnermuseum.org

THE LOVE TREE CAFÉ

All that we love deeply becomes a part of us.
—Helen Keller, The Story of My Life

The love tree towers over the Love Tree Café, on the thoroughfare of Cordova Street, and stands congruent to the Tolomato Cemetery. There are many stories about lovers and intertwined trees, but the haunted love tree of St. Augustine simultaneously beckons and inhibits the romantic attachments of lovers who flock to the site.

Diane Lane, proprietor of the Love Tree Café, presides over the lofty spectacle from her turquoise and yellow café, where a sable palm tree, several stories high, grows out of a live oak tree. If the trees separate, each dies. Lane passes out printed copies of the love tree legend, which has no documented source. The legend states that two lovers planted two trees to express their devotion:

> *The woman planted a palm tree, which was sturdy and able to withstand the most violent storms. The man planted an oak tree representing flexibility and protection. Apparently, when the lovers passed away, the legend says, their love endured the passage of death…as a manifestation of their joining together for eternity, the oak tree, wrapped around the slender palm tree, protecting her while she stood steadfast.*

The famous love tree, with a palm visibly growing out of an oak.

If this tale sounds a little fantastic, keep in mind that the tree has been in place for many years, at least since the nineteenth century. Before the building was the Love Tree Café, it was Millie's Sandwich Shop and, before that, an antique store. Before that, it may well have been there prior to the

Tolomato Cemetery. According to Charles Tingley of the St. Augustine Historical Society, on some eighteenth-century maps, there used to be a cathedral in the vicinity, which may have stood where the café now resides. It is likely that the Love Tree Café was built over an old Indian village, its church and the consequent remains of its inhabitants. Tingley says, "Old graveyards associated with churches could have burial grounds that extended as far as Artillery Lane."

How does love and death mesh in the love tree legend? Does the famous tree spring from a lover's grave? There are, in fact, many documented stories about the mystical connections between man's origin and demise and the role of trees. In *The Grail Legend* by Emma Jung, she writes of the baby Jesus depicted as the top of a tree, growing out of the body of Adam. According to J.H. Philpot in her book *The Sacred Tree*, published in 1897, "There is little doubt that most…races regarded the tree as the home haunt or embodiment of a spiritual essence." Ovid, in *Metamorphosis*, often turns people into plants and trees.

THEN AND NOW

The wood-frame shingled building where the Love Tree Café now resides was built in 1923. On the *St. Johns County Property Appraiser Map*, the café abuts the Tolomato Cemetery, lending credence to the notion that at one time its land was part of the cemetery.

To enter, customers climb wooden porch steps and step over pine wood floors to a back room, where they can find Tammy Chapman, a paranormal investigator who rents a room from Lane to sell candy. She claims to have had a few paranormal experiences in the building.

Customers wishing to avoid spirits can keep walking to a pleasant, shady outdoor porch where the food is served. The Love Tree Café dishes up reasonably priced salads and sandwiches; the Lumberjack sandwich and the Love Tree homemade chili are popular favorites. A lone couple, settling the bill, praised the food and the atmosphere. "We just came up for the day," they said, "to walk around and enjoy the day. This was great."

There is a Kiddo's section on the menu, and no alcohol is served. The menu itself, a folded paper brochure, features a cover silhouette of an oak tree with a topknot crown of palm fronds. In stenciled script, it proclaims, "I kissed someone special…under The Love Tree."

This is the last part of Lane's legend, which wistfully plays out the exchange of true love's kiss under the love tree. Presumably, people who lock lips under the hybrid tree stay together forever. "All of the tours go to the love tree. I warn people to be careful," Lane says. "Don't kiss your kids."

Love Tree Café
6 Cordova Street
St. Augustine, Florida, 32804
http://www.lovetreecafe.com

MURDER ON MARINE STREET

To reopen the case would be to pursue an innocent person.
—St. Johns County sheriff Dudley Garret, Florida Times-Union, *1976*

A Lindsley Facebook friend, Noah Taylor, posted the following brief story about the house on 124 Marine Street:

> *Stories about Athalia Ponsell Lindsley? I have a very chilling one. A few years ago, at night, my father and I walked by the house. A black cat streaked across the street right in front of us and walked to the very step where she was hacked to death and stopped and stared at us. It's true and gave us chills.*

THEN AND NOW

The 1974 murder of Athalia Ponsell Lindsley is documented in a self-published book, available at some ghost kiosks, titled *Bloody Sunset in St. Augustine.* It was written by Jim Mast, a journalist, and Nancy Powell, a friend of the murder victim and a former St. Augustine news bureau manager for the *Florida Times Union* in Jacksonville. The book is expensive and is a combination, according to reviews, of fact and fiction.

A Facebook site is dedicated to the unsolved case of the murder victim, and it contains all of the downloaded court documents and newspaper clippings about the murder. The St. Augustine Historical Research Library has another file of thick clippings. The facts of the case are simple, yet the murder remains unsolved.

Athalia Ponsell Lindley, a former model, inventor, author, dancer and television game show hostess, moved to the 124 Marine Street mansion in St. Augustine in 1972. The house was her inheritance and the home of her mother whom she nursed through a long terminal illness.

In St. Augustine, Athalia practiced real estate and married a former mayor, James "Jinx" Lindsley. She also began a feud with her next-door neighbor, Alan Stanford, a St. Johns County manager. Initially, the dispute concerned her barking dogs, but it expanded, on Athalia's side, to Stanford's credentials, job performance and salary. Eventually, the feud escalated. Athalia and Stanford both called newspapers trying to discredit each other. Athalia thought Stanford was incompetent and wanted him fired from his position as county manager. Alan Stanford allegedly threatened Athalia's life.

These threats became chillingly relevant in the early evening of January 23, 1974, when Athalia was found partially decapitated on the steps of her 124 Marine Street residence. Four of the five main arteries to her brain had been severed with a machete-type weapon, and a neighbor described the scene as "solid blood." The blood splattered the white walls of her stucco home, and the impact of the murder weapon scarred a cast-iron porch railing. That blood led police on a trail from the steps of Athalia's front stoop to the garage of Stanford's house.

It would appear that Athalia's impatience with the competence of city officials, policies and procedures was well founded. Emergency medical technicians hosed down the murder site, effectively eliminating the murderer's footprints. Alan Stanford, who, along with his family, gave conflicting accounts of his whereabouts and activities at the time of the crime, was indicted a week later. Locke McCormick, another neighbor, and an eyewitness to the crime, identified Stanford as the murderer but later recanted. A county mechanic turned in a machete and a bloody bag containing a watch, a shirt, a belt and dark trousers that he pulled from a marsh. The contents were positively identified as belonging to Alan Stanford. Last, a machete was actually checked out from the county inventory months before and never returned. The signer, Alan Stanford, claimed it was lost.

In November of that year, Athalia's neighbor, Francis Bemis—a seventy-six-year-old retired journalist and another potential eyewitness—went out

The murder site of Athalia Ponsell Lindsley.

for her evening walk and was found the next day in a vacant lot with her skull bashed in.

The murder trial began in February 1975, lasted two weeks and the jury took two hours to find Stanford innocent. When he was acquitted, he fell to his knees and thanked God. After his acquittal, Stanford immediately moved out of St. Augustine, eventually settling in South Carolina. He never returned.

The house, which is still in a nice section of town, is accessible by sidewalk past the St. Augustine National Cemetery. The house itself is a two-story beige stucco with green trim, more than three thousand square feet and worth at least $500,000 in today's market. There is an arched doorway and grills on the windows. A flowered wreath hangs on the glass door. The landscaping and decoration is symmetrical, with two big identical flowerpots on either side of the infamous steps leading up to the stoop, two urns on either side of the door, plants and bushes on both sides of the house in the same positions. An ornate iron gate guards the backyard. There is a clear view of Matanzas Bay, but there is also new construction that will eventually obstruct the vista.

A young couple, arms twined around each other's waists, passed some tourists who gawked at the house. The man asked, "Is something going on?" A little shamefaced, the tourists admitted that they were sightseeing the site of murder. The couple became animated. "La fantasma!" the guy translated to his girlfriend.

"Can you feel something?" the girl asked, as her boyfriend averred, "Now I can feel the energy!" Perhaps "energy" is not the right word, but the discerning historian is definitely going to feel something when reviewing the news coverage of the murder.

On the afternoon of her last day among the living, the fifty-six-year-old Athalia had lunch with her husband and her friend Nancy Powell. January 23 was the Chinese New Year, and the well-read Athalia cut her fish with a fork because knives were considered bad luck on such a day. After lunch, she rode to Jacksonville with her husband and went shopping. Back in St. Augustine, they drove to a parking lot, where she kissed her husband goodbye and transferred groceries for a Chinese dinner into her classic Cadillac. She drove to her house, where she perused her mail on the front porch, keeping company with a lame blue jay named Clementine whom she'd rescued the year before. Then, according to someone's perspective, her time ran out. After Athalia was hacked to death, the blue jay Clementine was found in the bushes, a mash of pulverized feathers.

The most startling aspect of the murder, aside from Stanford's acquittal, was the press that the murder victim received after her death. One headline in the *St. Augustine Record* noted, "Obnoxious Victim Had No Shortage of Possible Killers." A former county commissioner, Herbie Wiles, went on the record describing the murder as "something that was a tragic, tragic thing. A poor, poor man was wrongfully accused." A local church actually set up a defense fund for Stanford, actively soliciting donations.

Years later, the vitriol concerning Athalia had not abated. A 1989 *St. Augustine Record* article titled, "A Woman of Mystery, Controversy, Charm," by Jackie Feagan opened with the following line: "Athalia Ponsell like the Cadillac she drove, was past her prime."

On Athalia's Facebook page, "friends" spar about the crime, trying to one up one another with their knowledge, insight or even proximity. After all, many people still alive in St. Augustine remember when it all happened and knew the people involved, although most are gone or unavailable. Stanford and his wife are dead. So is Jinx. Locke McCormick lives in Jacksonville and is not open to questions from journalists.

Athalia was an independent, educated, outspoken woman, and in the 1970s, she received the death penalty for her lack of discretion. So perhaps "energy" is indeed one way to describe the crime, the trial, the aftermath and the continuing controversy. Another way to describe it would be as a travesty of justice. Ghosts or no ghosts, that's enough to haunt the house for a good long time.

Athalia Ponsell Lindley
124 Marine Street
St. Augustine, Florida, 32084
https://www.facebook.com/#!/athalia.lindsley

O.C. WHITE'S SEAFOOD AND SPIRITS

When you are out of control, someone is ready to take over.
—*Toba Beta,* My Ancestor Was an Ancient Astronaut

S arah Abbott, an employee of O.C. White's Seafood and Spirits restaurant, has some things to say about "events" in the eatery that regularly occur under her watch. However, it is a weekend when we speak to her, and she is busy answering the phone and serving drinks. When she is free for a minute, she picks up the thread of an earlier conversation.

Sarah says hurriedly, "Candles relight after being blown out. Glassware flies off of glass racks." She claims to have actually seen these events. She said, "Oh, yeah. I got hit in the shoulder by a glass. There's chairs that after being stacked, fall back on the tables, uh, but really? The things that are seen? Are in the middle of the night. You know if the manager is here in the wee hours of the morning, he has walked out of the office and seen apparitions."

Sarah owns an eight- by ten-inch picture of the stairwell blanketed by a bank of vapor. "Just almost a fog. Of the original owner of the house. When it was privately owned."

Sarah is a sensible, hardworking woman. Misty apparitions, flying objects and spontaneous combustion—what the heck is going on at O.C. White's?

If its ghostly shenanigans are the antics of a former owner, then there is a long lineup of translucent suspects. According to Dave and Tom Lapham's book *Ancient City Hauntings: More Ghosts of St. Augustine,* there have been five

The spooky stairwell.

owners: a Spanish merchant, a widow of a famous general, an owner of a cigar factory, an owner of a wax museum and Dave White, the only owner who is actually breathing and above ground.

Which one is piqued enough to throw glassware hard enough to *boink* a bartender in the shoulder? It's not Dave White. According to a lengthy interview he gave for the Laphams' book in 2004, he has been as startled by the strangeness in the house as his employees. In the book, he related experiences in the restaurant of spontaneous combustion, strange odors, a door on the third floor that locks and unlocks at will, footsteps on the second floor, tinkling wine glasses and dancing salt and pepper shakers.

There are too many other accounts of the unaccountable to discount the stories out of hand. The desk clerk at next-door Marion Motor Lodge often took a 3:00 a.m. stroll down Cadiz Street, a narrow alley that divides the lodge from the restaurant. During his walk, he smelled smoke and heard taps on the darkened windows of the second floor of O.C. White's.

Even regular guidebooks, such as Rajtar and Goodman's meticulous *Guide to Historic St. Augustine*, refer to the restaurant as haunted.

Who haunts the house? Any one of its former owners, his descendants or guests would qualify. Is it Miguel Ysnardy, the royal treasurer of the second Spanish period? Was it the widow of a famous general, Margaret Worth, who renovated the home and lived there for so many years alone? Was it Pantaleon Felix Carcaba, the independent cigar factory owner, who belonged to two secret societies? Was it his son and heir, William Henry Carcaba, who was shot to death on the other side of town? Is it a former member of the Benevolent and Protective Order of the Elks? Was it George Potter, the midwestern wax museum owner who relocated the house, coquina brick by brick, from what is now its parking lot to its bayside locale? Is it one of its former guests when it functioned as a hotel for almost fifty years?

Or is it all of them?

Locals hear mysterious tapping on the windows late at night at O.C. White's Seafood and Spirits.

THEN AND NOW

O.C. White's has a string of illustrious owners, all important to the history of St. Augustine. The building would clearly be a museum if it were not a popular restaurant.

The first owner, Miguel Ysnardy, a prominent Spaniard, interpreter and the royal treasurer of the second Spanish period, built the white colonial-style house, formerly on 16 Marine Street, in 1791. There are just a few dozen of these original structures left in St. Augustine, and an old article in the *St. Augustine Record*, dated July 4, 1936, tells us why. The house is described at that time as "still sturdy" and "with no sign of weakness" despite numerous renovations. Rajtar and Goodman in their book speculate that Ysnardy used blocks of coquina of different sizes and shapes that he quarried from previously existing structures.

Regardless, Ysnardy inexplicably sold the house in 1799. As to his reasons for selling the house instead of willing it to his family, as most of his peers did, no record exists. Ysnardy speculated in cattle, so perhaps he needed the money. In fact, 1799 may have been a lean year for Ysnardy, who tried to raise more cash by submitting a petition to the governor, claiming to own a portion of Tolomato Cemetery. Ysnardy proposed relocating the Tolomato dead, at the church's expense, and using the land for his own "cultivation." His petition was unsuccessful, but as a side note, Ysnardy did stake some sanctified land eventually, in 1803, when he died and was buried in the St. Augustine cathedral—one of only three people ever to repose there.

In any case, Ysnardy sold the house on Marine Street as a commercial property, and it functioned as a hotel until the mid-nineteenth century. The year Ysnardy sold the house is the year its next owner was born. Margaret Worth, widow of General William Worth and the mother-in-law of Governor Sprague, purchased the property sometime after 1849 and lived there alone until her daughter and her son-in-law, the governor of the Reconstruction era, moved in. Then the house became livelier and the center of all social functions in post–Civil War St. Augustine. Worth died in 1869, and her daughter, Margaret, owned the house until 1904, when she sold it to Pantaleon Felix (P.F.) Carcaba, whose descendants still live in St. Augustine.

P.F. Carcaba is famous for opening the first cigar factory in St. Augustine. Tampa clearly had the coastline for tobacco shipments, yet Carcaba gave serious competition to the Tampa cigar monopoly. He traveled regularly to Havana to buy tobacco and tried growing it in St. Augustine. Perhaps he also stored it in the house on 16 Marine Street, as many of the paranormal events at O.C. White's involve smoke, odors and fire.

Much more likely, though, is that Carcaba used the house for meetings of his Elks Lodge, which was chartered in St. Augustine around the time he bought the property. Carcaba had illustrious connections through his membership in two benevolent secret societies, the Elks and the Knights of Pythias. Both are service organizations with secret oaths and rituals, conducive to spooky haunting. In fact, after P.F. Carcaba sold the house, the Elks owned it until it was sold in 1948 to its next owner, George L. Potter.

Potter was the original owner of the first wax museum in the United States, which is housed on King Street today. A widower, Potter began his collection of wax figures while he owned the house on 16 Marine Street. It is likely that he stored the lifelike replicas of historic figures and celebrated people in the house on Marine Street as well.

By 1960, however, the house had fallen into disrepair and, because of renovations, barely resembled the structure built by Ysnardy. Potter razed it and then rebuilt it with the original materials and in its original colonial design at its present location on 118 Avenida Menéndez. The mansion overlooks the City Yacht Marina and the historic Bridge of Lions. The former location of the house serves as a free parking lot for the restaurant.

David White bought the building in the early 1990s and christened it O.C. (Out of Control) White's.

A mysterious fire in 1992 almost destroyed the second and third floors of the restaurant. White rebuilt, and the restaurant is a popular favorite in the ancient city.

Many people have eaten at O.C. White's for years without knowing its history, although the typed narrative is printed on its menu. Its square footage is just over three thousand feet. The restaurant features a patio, a first-floor bar and

The bayside locale of O.C. White's.

a main staircase that leads to the second-floor dining room and the balcony. For patrons dining on the breezy balcony, the restaurant affords a view of the bay and a view of the city, retaining a festive, convivial atmosphere. The seafood menu is extensive, featuring gator tail, steamers, conch fritters, coconut shrimp and crab cakes. Dancing salt and pepper shakers aside, the seasoning is superb.

As far as the "spirits" of the restaurant are concerned, their combined history adds context to the rich historic content of the structure. One could say that the departed hosts of O.C. White's are a little "Out of Control," using employees for target practice with the glassware. Still, in St. Augustine, tourists and locals who want to be at the heart of things, past and present, head for O.C. White's.

O.C. White's
118 Avenida Menéndez
St. Augustine, Florida, 32084-4403
http://www.ocwhitesrestaurant.com

THE SPANISH MILITARY HOSPITAL MUSEUM

Listen there to their lamentations, and remedy all their miseries, afflictions and sorrows.
—*Eduardo Chávez,* Our Lady of Guadalupe and Saint Juan Diego

Tourists can go to St. Augustine perhaps one hundred times and never notice Aviles Street, a narrow roadway with overhanging balconies. It is a tourist warren of cafés, with an art gallery and a candle shop. It is also the location of the Spanish Military Hospital Museum. Enter and stand in the dim room facing a counter filled with brochures. Speak to the wrinkled, stooped employee dressed in a nineteenth-century costume who comes out and says in a gravelly voice, "You can't work here and not have a ghostly experience. This is a certified haunted building."

Local lore supports her claim, although the building itself is actually reconstructed on the site of the original structure. Still, so much horror, death and anguish occurred on this location that ghost stories sound plausible. According to Lapham's *Ghosthunting in Florida*, beds in the Spanish Military Hospital Museum move around on their own, strange noises occur and crucifixes are flung onto the floor. Diane Lane, a local merchant, tells this story, currently making the rounds with the "paranormals," about an event that occurred to a tourist:

> *On a ghost tour, this woman came into the hospital. And what we do is, we take people into these different rooms, and we tell you strange things that have happened in the rooms. This woman, I guess she was*

feeling some empathy, so to herself, she asked the question, "Is there anyone here?"

The next morning, she was at her hotel, and she was getting dressed, and her husband said to her, "What is that on your back?" They looked on her back, and it was, mirror image, the word "Yes" imprinted on her back. So, she came back to the hospital, and she showed us the small part of her back, and we saw it. By the time she left, it had faded away, but...she got her answer. They were telling her, yes, there's someone there.

THEN AND NOW

According to a 1937 article in the *St. Augustine Record*, "First Hospital Established in This Old City," the Old Spanish Military Hospital Museum was once known as Our Royal Hospital of Our Lady Guadalupe. It served only sick, wounded or dying Spanish military men during the second Spanish period at the turn of the nineteenth century. Historic tours of the hospital museum emphasize the primitive medical conditions and the ghastly consequences of these ineffective treatments on helpless soldiers.

The cobblestone streets cover a mass grave of Spanish soldiers.

So distinguishing a feature was the hospital during the second Spanish period that Aviles Street, where the restored building is located, was known as "Hospital Street." The restored hospital was resurrected as a museum in the 1960s.

Then, in the 1970s, during the repair of a water line, the city made a ghastly discovery: the cobblestone street outside the hospital covered a mass graveyard.

Buried right outside the door of the Old Spanish Military Hospital Museum are hundreds of human skeletons, as well as the amputated bones of Spanish soldiers' arms, legs and feet. After an examination by archaeologists, the city simply returned the bones to their makeshift grave, where they remain to this day. In order to enter the museum, visitors literally walk over the mass grave of the Spanish soldiers who once languished inside.

The museum is small, less than 1,700 square feet. The tour consists of an examination of four rooms: the ward, the apothecary, the surgeons' room and the mourning room. Visitors see the instruments of surgery and hear in gory detail the common practice of amputation without anesthetics—hence the multitude of partial bones in the mass grave right outside the entrance. The mourning room, where patients were brought to die, is supposed to be particularly haunted; it contained the fear and anguish of dying soldiers forced to listen to the sawing and hammering of their own coffins, which were constructed in the same room.

St. Johns County property records code the museum as a tourist attraction with a University of Florida mailing address. As an educational museum, the building has a state exemption and pays no taxes. Various tours are offered, including educational field trips during the day and ghost tours at night. A good collection of guide and history books about St. Augustine is for sale in the main entrance.

It is an interesting tour for the serious St. Augustine visitor, bent on discovering where, how and why medicine was practiced in the late eighteenth century. The branded tourist's question about whether spirits are *here* misses the point. Mortal bones located just below the telling of ghostly tales validate the fact that scores of some ones are indeed *there*.

Old Spanish Military Hospital Museum
3 Aviles Street
St. Augustine, Florida, 32084
http://www.spanishmilitaryhospital.com

RIPLEY'S BELIEVE IT OR NOT! MUSEUM

I do not know how anyone can live without some small place of enchantment to turn to.
—Marjorie Kinnan Rawlings

Violette Avino sells tickets at Ripley's Believe It or Not! Museum, and she's been doing it for a year and a half. Violette hasn't seen or heard any ghosts, although she knows some stories and a lot of the history associated with the museum, back when it was know as Warden Castle:

> *This building was finished in 1887 as a private home for William Warden—a big honcho of Standard Oil partnered along with Rockefeller and Flagler. This was his winter home. It was many acres, all the way up to the fort* [Castillo de San Marcos]. *He lived here with his family until the Great Depression came along.*
>
> *Then it was vacant for years. Vagrants were living here, and the City of St. Augustine condemned it; they wanted to burn it to the ground. But it was put out for a bid, and Marjorie Kinnan Rawlings, who wrote* The Yearling *and* Cross Creek, *bought it in the '40s and turned it into a hotel and kept a penthouse on the fourth floor. It became a hotel for socialites. In 1944, there was a fire on the third and fourth floors, and two women died of smoke asphyxiation. People heard screams and a commotion; people saw smoke, and then the women were found dead in their bathtubs.*
>
> *Two or three rooms of the museum have a large concentration of energy in the same area where the women were found. We have these old-time*

picture machines there that take coins, and people say all the time that someone pushes them, like "Get outta the way." Just in working at the museum, I've seen lights shut on and off, the volume on some of the exhibits goes up unexpectedly. Then again, it's an old building. We could blame it on the wiring.

Sightings of the women's ghosts are documented on the Ripley's website, and customers usually see one or the other of them from an outside window. Former employees also report the occasional odor of smoke wafting from the third and fourth floors.

THEN AND NOW

At the turn of the nineteenth century, William Warden was known as an "oil swell" and was one of the multimillionaires who belonged to the elite club of Standard Oil stockholders. He built the thirteen-thousand-square-feet of Warden Castle for his family of sixteen, and Warden lived there until the 1930s.

During the Depression, squatters overran the poured concrete castle, committing crimes, even murder. Pulitzer Prize–winning author Marjorie Kinnan Rawlings and her husband, Norton Baskin, saved the structure by purchasing it in 1941 and naming it Castle Warden Hotel. Rawlings maintained a penthouse on the fourth floor, and a good friend of hers, Ruth Hopkins Pickering, stayed there at Rawlings's insistence. Apparently, Pickering, a lifelong St. Augustine resident and the former wife of a reporter with the *Chicago Sun*, was experiencing some domestic problems, and Rawlings, ironically as it turned out, felt that her hotel was the safest place for her.

According to the coroner's report, "a fire of unknown origin" demolished a third- and a fourth-floor room. The rooms belonged to Pickering and a Florida State graduate, Betty Richeson, in her twenties, who checked in ninety minutes before the fire. Both women suffocated from the smoke, and officials speculated that the origin could have been a smoldering cigarette on the third floor. On the other hand, it could have been something more sinister, and the fire was set to cover up a crime. Rawlings was devastated by the death of her good friend, and she sold the building six years later to Robert L. Ripley's estate. A new

Exterior of the entrance and the distinctive canopy at Ripley's oddities museum.

building of almost eight thousand square feet was added to house Ripley's "odditorium" collection.

Thus, Ripley's touring compendium of oddities found its first permanent home in a haunted castle worth about $1.5 million, minus the contents, in today's market. The famous Ripley's canopy leads to a gift shop, prospects of Ripley's ghost tours after dark, sightseeing trains and more than eight hundred exhibits. Frequent visitors flock to the Degas work *L'Absinthe* made entirely of burnt toast and Botticelli's *The Birth of Venus* composed of lint.

The guy with the candle growing out of his head isn't bad either, although considering the history of Warden Castle, he should definitely pack a fire extinguisher.

Ripley's Believe It or Not! Museum
19 San Marco Avenue
St. Augustine, Florida, 32084
http://www.ripleys.com/staugustine

SCARLETT O'HARA'S BAR
AND RESTAURANT

I'll never be hungry again.
—*Scarlett O'Hara,* Gone With the Wind

On a rainy summer evening, tourists and locals wander into the open-air bar at Scarlett O'Hara's on Hypolita Street. Raina, a bartender in a black tank top and black shorts, serves wings and tells patrons about the former owner of the house who drowned in a bathtub and haunts the upstairs men's room of the restaurant. "If you want more information," she says, "come back in the morning and speak to Tom, Captain Tom. He can tell a lot more."

Captain Tom Brown has worked the day shift at Scarlett O'Hara's Bar and Restaurant for twenty-five years. He's also a pirate reenactor for an event called "The Golden Age of Piracy," which is associated with the St. Augustine Pirate and Treasure Museum. There is some irony here; although he wears a long brown ponytail, Captain Tom is mild-mannered, soft-spoken and not at all reminiscent of the bloodthirsty rogues he routinely imitates.

His ghost story is scary enough, though. It entails a man named George Colee, who built the cedar and cypress building on Hypolita as a private residence for his fiancée. She left him before he could finish because she was dating one of the soldiers at the fort. There was an altercation on St. George Street between the soldier and George. Within a few weeks, George was found drowned in the bathtub upstairs, where the men's room is now. Captain Tom suspects foul play.

The bathtub at Scarlett O'Hara's was used as a salad bar at one time and later as a couch. But today, "The bathtub is gone," said Captain Tom. He offers no explanation. Elaborating about the ghost, he says:

> *He's upstairs in the Ghost Bar. You never see him. He'll tap you on the shoulder, especially if you're in the urinal, or he'll blow on the back of your neck. If a waitress leaves napkins on a table, she'll return to find them fanned out. We don't have candles up there anymore because he lights all the candles. Once he shoved a cop, who will no longer go upstairs.*
>
> *We have a picture of him upstairs with a crack in the canvas going through his face. Sometimes the crack widens; sometimes it narrows. He is particular about where his picture is hung because he wants to see people. If it's not in the right spot, the picture falls to the floor. It was on the stairwell, and they took out the stairwell, and then they hung his picture behind a door—with two screws—and every morning it would be on the floor. He likes where he is now, upstairs in the Ghost Bar.*

Captain Tom says there is another spirit in the building on the north side: a dark, slender man who walks through the dining room day and night. He mentions that all the spirits hate cursing, which is a similar peccadillo present in the Catalina ghost story at Harry's Seafood Bar and Grille.

Customers must climb a steep staircase to check out the Ghost Bar. Chairs are parked with their rungs in the air on square glass-topped tables. There are posters of Vivien Leigh and Clark Gable on the walls and a mounted flat-screen TV, with condiments and Styrofoam containers piled up on a shelf underneath.

There is also the portrait of some nineteenth-century gentleman, presumably George, mounted on a brick column. A small light bulb shines from the hood of the picture frame on the faded likeness of an unsmiling young man with his hair parted in the middle. The crack across his face is fairly wide, probably something to do with the humidity.

There is a sign: "Welcome to the Ghost Bar." One wonders how much spirits, the alcoholic kind, have to do with the intangible spirits of haunted repute. For example, if anyone shoved a police officer, accidentally or otherwise, the shover would be happy to have a ghost on hand to blame.

THEN AND NOW

There are really two restaurants on Hypolita Street: Scarlett O'Hara's and Rhett's. They're sister restaurants with different menus; Rhett's is a little more upscale. Both establishments comprise the former Colee dwelling. There was an east side and a west side, and the Florida master site file lists the date of origin as 1879. The site file also notes that George Colee shared the home with his adult son, William. Genealogical records indicate that George had three other sons in addition to William: James, George and Charles. All of them married, had children and lived to ripe old ages.

The Colee family also founded the St. Augustine Transfer Company, which was responsible for all the horse and buggies on the streets of St. Augustine—in those days for transportation, nowadays for sightseeing.

The Colees lived in the house on Hypolita until 1924. Then it was a funeral home until Barry Gaines and Kevin Finch purchased it in the '70s, completely remodeled the interior and added a porch, which they lined with rocking chairs. The bars downstairs and upstairs are impressive constructions of hand-carved mahogany, as old as the house and a part of a former bedroom suite from New Orleans.

Sign for the restaurant visible from Hypolita Street.

John Arbiennez owns the restaurant today, and it is not a franchise, although an ill-fated expansion was opened in New Orleans right around the time of Hurricane Katrina. In St. Augustine, Scarlett O'Hara's Bar and Restaurant is a popular watering hole for locals as well as tourists. Go early on a Friday night if you want to get in, go late if you want to stand in a long line most of the evening.

As to the story of George Colee, there is no substantive evidence that he was ever a jilted cuckold or that he drowned in a bathtub. There is no real evidence that the picture in the Ghost Bar bears the visage of the real George Colee, although Captain Tom says that his great-grandniece wanted it at some point. However, the Scarlett O'Hara Bar and Restaurant ghost story is pervasive. It appears in the National Directory of Haunted Places, on various websites and in books on ghostly lore.

Perhaps there is some truth to any ghost story that has grown, changed and mutated during a century's worth of telling and retelling. If you want to have some fun and some good food, Scarlett O'Hara's can cook up all that and a ghost on the side.

Scarlett O'Hara's Bar and Restaurant
70 Hypolita Street
St. Augustine, Florida, 32084
http://www.scarlettoharas.net

St. Augustine Lighthouse
and Museum

Dark of the Moon Tour

How far that little candle throws its beams.
—*William Shakespeare,* The Merchant of Venice

To understand the St. Augustine Lighthouse, one needs a foundation in its ghostly history. Of this, there is no shortage. Karen Harvey, St. Augustine historian and author, reported in *The Compass* in 1990 that David Swain, the St. Augustine Lighthouse keeper from 1933 until 1944, had many ghost stories. He told of restorers working on scaffolding inside the lighthouse, putting up pigeon blocks and looking up to see the translucent image of someone hanging there. He told of walking from the keeper's house to the tower and hearing footsteps following him to the top and back. He said he "could hear the rocks a crunching."

The most famous ghost story originates from a well-documented tragedy that occurred in 1873 to Hezekiah Pittee's family. Working as the superintendent of lighthouse construction, his job entailed building lighthouses along the East Coast. The original St. Augustine Lighthouse, constructed of coquina, was built in the early nineteenth century. It was too close to the water, and beach erosion ensured that it was eventually washed away. Pittee was in charge of the lighthouse that stands today, and he arrived in 1871 to begin working on it. He also brought his four children: Eliza, fifteen; Mary, twelve; Keri, four; and Edward, eight.

Unfortunately for the children, Pittee's construction workers had a handcart that extended about two hundred yards along a rail down to an

The lighthouse before sundown—Hezekiah Pittee's creation.

inlet. At the water's edge, there was a gate to stop the handcart. When a ship would come in, they'd load things onto the cart and take it back to the construction site.

On July 10, the Pittee kids, along with a ten-year-old female friend, piled into the cement handcart, rode it down the rail to the gate and flipped it over into the water, which pinned all the kids underneath. One of the construction workers ran down and rescued the little ones Keri and Edward, but he couldn't save the others. They drowned. In spite of his awful tragedy, Pittee finished the lighthouse and left town. According to legend, something ghostly lingered.

Ever since those girls passed away, people have seen them. They see the girls walking in the neighborhood and playing across the street on the swings; they see them in the lighthouse and running along the grounds. They've heard them whispering and singing.

In the old days, people ran away from ghosts screaming. Nowadays, tourists pay to catch a glimpse of them.

THEN AND NOW

Although there are many old ghost stories concerning the St. Augustine Lighthouse, its popular "Dark of the Moon" tour is always trying to conjure up new ones. Hopefully their plan does not entail the ghosts of tour guests eternally tripping down the 219 steps of the lighthouse, as the tour takes place around 8:30 p.m., in total darkness, except for some glow stick necklaces provided free of charge after the twenty-five-dollar admission fee. It is much more likely that tour guides hope fervently for something, currently in the paranormal realm, to occur during an actual tour. For an additional fee, guests rent EVP (electronic voice phenomenon) boxes with paranormal playback that light up with any random musings a ghost may care to offer.

There are about fifty people in each tour, including men, women, teenagers and children. "Dark of the Moon" tours take place on Friday, Saturday and Sunday nights, and children as young as seven are allowed to come. There is a nine-year-old girl in the throng who clings to her mother throughout the tour.

It begins outside the gift shop, and then the tour guides divide the guests into two groups; one climbs to the top of the lighthouse—in total darkness—and the other visits the darkened keeper's house, the museum and the lighthouse basement. To make it an authentic nineteenth-century experience, apparently, there is no air conditioning in any of these facilities.

One group begins at the foot of the lighthouse, and the tour guide, Ben, spends some time telling everyone about how on one tour, he saw a ghostly hand reach through the door. A tour guest states that on a previous tour, he heard singing. Someone else mentions seeing kids in old-fashioned garb running through the woods. The guides keep talking about previous tours when the EVPs "lit up and went crazy." During most tours, however, this does not occur.

Inside the close quarters of the lighthouse, teenagers sprint up the stairs, and adults follow until all emerge at the top, wheezing, to a refreshing breeze 165 feet above the ground with a panoramic view of Anastasia Island in darkness punctuated by some house lights. Despite the twelve-foot automated Fresnel lens with its 370 hand-cut prisms, it is clear that visibility at night is strictly a one-way beacon for ships at sea.

Then it is time to descend the steps and trek on to the keeper's house, which used to be a duplex. The north side was where the keeper lived; the south side was where the assistant lived. Sometimes there'd be another assistant up in the attic. Tourists sit in a semicircle of folding chairs in the Pittee girls' old bedroom. Ben tells everyone that sometimes, for fun, the girlish ghosts tie the laces of tour guests' shoes together so that they trip upon alighting, presumably cracking their heads on the wooden floor and joining the girls for an eternity of pranks in their ghostly realm.

The famous Fresnel lighthouse lens.

Alas, that seldom occurs either, so everyone troops downstairs to the museum and hears about how, on other tours, chairs moved around. Ben picks up and drops a wooden chair to demonstrate the loud noise it made when moved by paranormal sources. Then he takes everyone down to the basement, where he sits cross-legged in a semicircle and waits for something to happen. Something does happen. The chair in the room above scrapes on the floor. Ben springs into action on his hand-held radio

Museum and former lighthouse keeper's quarters.

and inquires of the other guide whether there are guests in the museum—meaning paying guests, not ectoplasm or, God forbid, someone making off with an elaborate ship model. The noise, as it turns out, is just some guests wandering around the museum in the dark, bumping into the chairs. Ben breathes a visible sigh of relief.

Back on the grounds, guests are invited to roam around in the dark, but given the toe-stubbers and the uneven terrain, most elect to leave, dragging with them the children and teenagers who thought the whole thing was really cool and totally authentic. Adults agreed that it was cool, although not literally, and as to its authenticity, at least as far as the ghosts are concerned, no one has any idea.

Although the St. Augustine Lighthouse is listed in both the National Register of Historic Places and on the National Directory of Haunted Places, it is clear that the lighthouse itself is an epicenter of pride and communality for St. Johns County. There is an annual lighthouse festival in March, and prestigious organizations, such as the Lighthouse Archaeological Maritime Program, utilize the museum to provide an impressive educational resource.

Tourists often sit on the west side of the Castillo de San Marcos at night and watch the beam of the lighthouse lengthen across the bay. A lighthouse is just a structure, after all, one that can crumble or need replacement. As a symbol, it does not tell much, but its light is another story. Its light can illuminate the present, or it can extend into the past and the future.

St. Augustine Lighthouse and Museum
81 Lighthouse Avenue
St. Augustine, Florida, 32080
http://www.staugustinelighthouse.com/events/darkofmoon.html

St. Augustine Old Jail

Be thine own palace, or the world's thy jail.
—*John Donne,* Verse Letter to Sir Henry Wotton

Kim Jones, the desk clerk at the Casablanca Inn, used to be a tour guide at the St. Augustine Old Jail. "It was the most inhuman jail," Kim said. "Most inmates didn't last a year." Her ghost story about the old jail concerns a tour she gave one rainy day:

> *It was more than rainy. There was thunder; there was lightening. Ghosts… that kind of weather brings them out. On the third floor, I saw a guy with a shaven head leave the cellblock. Shortly thereafter, the sixty-five-pound iron door creaked shut on its own. But I wasn't fazed. So much paranormal stuff goes on in this town that ghosts are an occupational hazard.*

Then and Now

Tourists used to mistake the St. Augustine Old Jail on San Marco Avenue for a hotel. According to Jones, that's because it was designed and paid for by Henry Flagler in 1888. He wanted the county jail as far away from his grand Hotel Ponce de Leon as possible. He went to the county demanding that it relocate the jail, and the county said no. He went down again and

Left: A creepy jail door that slams shuts by itself.

Below: Exterior of the jail built by Henry Flagler.

brought $10,000. The county said, "Yes, sir, Mr. Flagler, where would you like the jail?"

The pink Romanesque Revival jail, exactly one mile from Flagler College, the former Ponce hotel, is the result of Flagler's machinations. The jail was built by the Pauly Company, the same outfit that built the Old Clay County Jail in Green Cove Springs and Alcatraz in San Francisco. The original concrete floors, cells, bars, walls, kitchen and the sheriff's living quarters have all been preserved for a thriving tourist trade, which includes an after-dark ghost tour.

Since the St. Augustine Old Jail donated all of its papier-mâché prisoner mannequins to the Old Clay County jail, prisoner reenactors in striped jail garb conduct the day tours. One tour guide, "Willy," stays in character and claims to be a trustee who was thrown in jail for three years because of a drunken brawl at a local saloon. Then he fills the tour group in on the history of the jail.

It opened in 1891, and Sheriff Joe Perry ran it. He was the son of a fire and brimstone Baptist preacher from Alabama, and he was also a mountain of a man who stood six-foot-six and weighed three hundred pounds. "Behavioral correction" resulted in a few hours in the stockade or twenty-four hours in "the bird cage," a life-size lightweight cage strung with rope and slung over a tree limb, where the prisoner was forced to stand upright, dangling in the air, until Sheriff Perry said he could come down. There was also a jail cell for solitary confinement, a lockdown with no window and no light, where men were chained to the floor amid the rats and cockroaches.

Sheriff Perry was so dedicated to his job that he created living quarters at the jail for himself, his wife and their two daughters. He did not worry about their safety because he ran the jail with an iron hand, and even minor indiscretions by the prisoners resulted in brutal consequences.

Neon sign advertising the popular tourist attraction, day and night.

Interior of jail cells.

Sheriff Joe Perry.

Replica of the original gallows at the old jail.

The St. Augustine Old Jail was a hanging jail, and the condemned men lived on death row in a cell that faced the gallows. Officially, eight men died on the gallows, but there may have been "unofficial" hangings as well. The sheriff forced all of the inmates to watch the executions. There's a black-

and-white picture mounted on the wall of the old cell that depicts Sheriff Joe Perry putting a noose around a condemned man's neck.

There was no running water, but inmates were allowed to bathe once a month in one tub of water, which they lined up to use, one at a time. A bucket in the cell represented the toilet, and waste was thrown out the barred windows. Male inmates worked on chain gangs as unpaid farm laborers, with their legs shackled and a sixty-pound "ball and chain" attached. There were only two cells for female inmates, who cooked, cleaned and did the laundry. Meals consisted of coffee and beans, occasionally a few greens from the garden the inmates tended and, on rare occasions, 'possum or squirrel.

All inmates worked twelve hours a day, seven days a week. If a prisoner fell ill, he was sent to the infirmary, which was just another cell, where he languished until he died. Relatives had to claim the body within three days, or the corpse was sent to the potter's field—an indeterminate area that no one knows how to locate today. Death was the only escape from the jail before time was served. Sheriff Perry ensured that anyone who left prematurely never lived to tell the tale. The jail closed in 1953, and in 1987, it was added to the National Register of Historic Places.

Kim, the desk clerk at the inn, says that the ghosts of the old jail are nocturnal creatures and that night is the time to hear the disembodied groans, moans and menace of the departed prisoners. These were not good men by any stretch of the imagination; one prisoner sliced his wife's face up with a razor blade. Still, having done hard time in life, it seems particularly hellish to be confined to prison for an afterlife.

St. Augustine Old Jail
167 San Marco Avenue
St. Augustine, Florida, 32084

THE AUTHENTIC OLD DRUGSTORE

…whatever you might do elsewhere,
In the time remaining, you might do here.
—"Drugstore," poem by Carl Dennis

There is a widely circulated ghost tour story about the Authentic Old Drugstore that is embellished by a wonderful piece of folk art known as the marker of Chief Tolomato.

The tombstone sits inside the drugstore, which presumably sits atop the burial ground where the "chief" was laid to rest. A facsimile of an Indian head sits atop some cement pilings, held up with wedged cardboard, and bears a crude sign that reads:

NOTIS
THIS WERRY ELABORATE
PILE
IS ERECTED IN MEMERY OF
TOLOMATO
A SEMINOLE INGINE CHEEF WHOOS WIGWARM STUUD ON
THIS SPOT AND SIRROUNDINGS
WEE CHERRIS HIS MEMERY AS
HE WAS A GOOD HARTED CHEEF
HE WOOD KNOT TAKE YOOUR
SKALP WITHOUT YOU BEGGED

HIM TO DO SO OR PADE HIM
SUM MUNNY
HE ALWAYS AKTED MORE
LIKE A CHRISTSUN GENTLE
MAN THAN A SAVAGE INGINE
LET HIM
R.I.P.

The truth, according to the caption of its picture in the Library of Congress, is that the kitschy tombstone was erected in the late nineteenth century by the Authentic Old Drugstore's original owner, Dr. Speissegger. His only intention was to mark the name change, initiated by Henry Flagler, of Tolomato Street to Cordova Street. Years later, his two grandsons, brothers who lived above the drugstore, used the tombstone to drum up business, claiming to have found the bones of Chief Tolomato. Today, Tolomato Street is a distant walkway past a parking lot, and the bones of the Tolomato tribal chief are in no way connected to the fake tombstone.

In fact, the only Tolomato Indian in history worthy of the name "chief" resided along the coast of Spanish Florida in what is now Georgia. The real Chief Tolomato was a seventeenth-century Indian prince known by his Spanish Christian name of Don Juanillo. He had a falling out with some Franciscan friars over his practice of polygamy, so he scalped them and burned their missions. Juanillo was killed and scalped along with his braves in a fierce battle with the Spanish somewhere on the Georgia coast between St. Andrews Sound and the Savannah River, nowhere near the Authentic Old Drugstore ("Early History of the Creek Indians and Their Neighbors").

True, the Tolomato Indians moved closer to St. Augustine more than a century later to evade British attacks. They lived there until 1763, when they, along with the Spanish, departed for Cuba. And there they stayed. Chief Tolomato, a "Christsun gentleman," is conspicuously missing from recorded lore.

Clearly, the tombstone is a bit of touristy fun. Yet Myra Schaeffer, the manager of the drugstore, claims that the in-store cameras "pick up stuff" such as "white forms, hundreds of them, coming through the double doors," which to the layperson looks like the store's globe lamps on fast-forward. To Schaeffer, they look like "icicles, and sometimes I can see a face." According to her, the ghostly shenanigans at the Authentic Old Drugstore don't stop there:

Chief Tolomato's headstone.

No one is anywhere near the herb jars—and they just go off and break. Spirit didn't like this girl who worked here. A pin flew off the counter and hit her. She found glass in her coat pocket. A friend of mine is psychic, and she says a little girl is here by the name of Adele. My coffee cups kept breaking until I got her one of her own with her name on it. We keep it on a low shelf so she can reach it. But it broke recently, and my coffee cups started toppling off my desk again. We have to get her another one.

Aside from enabling destructive phantoms, Schaeffer says she's never actually seen or heard anything unusual inside the Authentic Old Drugstore. That doesn't mean she isn't extremely susceptible of suggestion. "When we first opened back up, people wouldn't come in," she says gloomily. "There's a dark entity."

THEN AND NOW

The property on 31 Orange Street used to be called the Oldest Drugstore, and when that claim was debunked, it became the Authentic Old Drugstore. The St. Johns County property appraiser codes the Authentic Old Drugstore's at almost five thousand square feet as a tourist attraction—appropriately, since it is very much a commercial venture and always has been. Well, almost. Like the Love Tree Café, the parking lot of the Authentic Old Drugstore abuts Tolomato Cemetery. Early nineteenth-century maps of St. Augustine label the site as an Indian village, the last North American mainland location of the Tolomato tribe. There is a good possibility that the wooden drugstore actually sits atop its remains.

Today, the old drugstore is an herbal remedy outlet, a café and an ice cream parlor, with hexagon-shaped tables and questionable décor such as an old lobster trap doubling as a chicken coop tacked on the wall.

There are two parts to the drugstore: the old and the new. The old is the entrance built in 1875. The Authentic Old Drugstore maintains antique cash registers, the original mahogany cabinets, wooden floors and an immense wooden door separating the old building from the add-on.

There are antique pipes and a glass-enclosed display of some of the original drugstore items: Moxie soda, Zemacol skin lotion and Vaseline hair tonic. Standing near the entrance is a life-size cardboard facsimile of the

Exterior of the Authentic Old Drugstore.

Front entrance of the old drugstore and a poster of the Speissegger brothers, who lived upstairs.

Speissegger brothers and, of course, Chief Tolomato's tombstone. In the back are the herbs, in large glass canisters, the poultices, the soaps and the beauty products.

Items from the drugstore museum.

The café and ice cream store were added onto in the 1970s when the Harris Corporation took over. The present owners have sold off the remains of a gift shop, presumably to clear space for expanding the café. There is a feeling of transition about the Authentic Old Drugstore, as though it struggles, after all these years, to grasp its identity. It straddles the old and the new. Paranormal hot spot for the ghost tours? Prosaic herbal outlet? A place for tourists to grab a bite between sightseeing jaunts? A local ice cream joint? The lack of focus is charming, in its way, for a site so rich in history.

The Authentic Old Drugstore
31 Orange Street
St. Augustine, Florida, 32084

TOLOMATO CEMETERY

What is essential is invisible to the eye.
—Antoine de Saint-Exupéry, The Little Prince

According to Peter Gold, former barrister and current guide for St. Augustine Gold Tours, the Tolomato Cemetery is seriously haunted. "A mist regularly appears in here," he says. According to the ghost tours, so do the ghosts of dead priests Father Varela and Bishop Verot, although the mortuary chapel that once housed their bones is empty. Also, a transparent bride, another woman in white, sweeps through the grounds for reasons known only to her ghostly self. Then there's little Jamie Morgan.

Facing west, in the front of the cemetery, is a lonely little headstone engraved with the name of James Morgan, his date of birth and his date of death: exactly ten days after his fifth birthday on November 28, 1877. Gold said, "He died. We don't know the reason. We believe he fell from a tree because that's where he first appeared. But Jamie regularly appears to kids. He's been seen running between the graves and in the tree, swinging his legs."

There really was a James Morgan because his name appears in the St. Augustine Historical Society's document of *Lists of Deaths and/or Burials* (1800–1899) for Tolomato Cemetery: "Morgan, James F. (Child) Nov. 18 1872–28 November 1877." He was the son of E. Morgan and Agnes Morgan, who are not buried at Tolomato Cemetery, since it was closed to new burials in 1884. There is no doubt that it was extremely tragic and unlucky to lose their young son, Jamie, and it didn't end there for the Morgans. A two-year-old daughter, Agnes, and a seven-year-old son, Arthur, are buried in St. Augustine's La Leche Shrine Cemetery, located on the west bank of Mantanzas Bay. Both siblings of young Jamie died in April 1886. There are, however, no rumors of their restless spirits seeking companionship. Unlike poor Jamie, Agnes and Arthur Morgan have each other.

THEN AND NOW

The Huguenot and the Tolomato Cemeteries are within walking distance of each other, and all burials ceased in both cemeteries in 1884. The similarities, however, end there. The Tolomato Cemetery is almost a century older and designed only for Catholics. Unlike the Huguenot Cemetery's Protestant residents and tourists, the Tolomato's deceased inhabitants are diverse, including a Catholic bishop, governors, slaves, convicts and soldiers of every creed and nationality. Last, the Tolomato Cemetery is no haphazard bone yard hastily devised by the city fathers. It is the oldest planned cemetery in the United States, dating back to the second Spanish period of St. Augustine.

Before then, the cemetery site had been around since the sixteenth century, and as its name suggests, it was originally one of six small Indian villages, providing refuge as a Franciscan mission. There was a chapel, a burying ground and, according to the Tolomato Preservation Association, "a four-story coquina bell-tower on the east façade."

The Tolomato Cemetery's historic distinction occurred because of a formal plan for the cemetery created by the Spanish in 1811. Currently held by the Library of Congress, the cemetery plan called for a "fenced square of 109 feet front for Cemetery of St. Augustine of East Florida." The plan designated extraordinary precision in the size of the plots, the amount of space separating the graves, the location of the burial vaults, the color they should be and even the type of masonry work that should occur (as they say, the best-laid plans...). Susan Parker wrote in her 2002 article for the *St. Augustine Record*, "Winds, flood tides, disturbances by later burials and mourners, and slow but relentless deterioration with time doomed early, mostly wooden markers. Unmarked graves from St. Augustine's early years lie around our old town."

Almost half of the Tolomato Cemetery's one thousand recorded burials occurred between 1784 and 1809. That number comprises a great number

Little Jamie Morgan's marker.

of burials in a very small space over a relatively short period. In most cases, the graves of Tolomato Cemetery were staked with wooden crosses, which deteriorated. There are reports in the St. Augustine Historical Society cemetery records of "a forsaken burying ground…overrun with hens and dogs…full of weeds…and with broken and neglected tombs." One of the earliest recorded burial dates belongs to a fifteen-year-old girl, Elizabeth Forrester, who died on December 20, 1798. Convicts dug up and desecrated her grave and her body.

All of the remaining markers are irregularly spaced. There is also a record of at least one headstone segregated outside the southeast corner of the cemetery for a man who committed suicide and consequently couldn't be buried on sanctified Catholic ground. Today, his headstone is completely gone. Charles Tingley of the St. Augustine Historical Society recalled, "The road was widened. There are a lot of Tolomato residents whose feet now rest under the curb."

In 1977, the City of St. Augustine renovated the cemetery, but visiting hours are restricted to one day per month. Still, the effect of the restoration and of its beauty remains. Centuries-old trees and a wire fence guard the dead and their history. Many of the departed are entombed above ground, some with plain markers and others with more intricate stones surrounded by wrought-iron fences that tilt with age. There is a path from the fence running straight between the graves to a small chapel at the other end of the enclosure. The chapel is empty now, but at one time, it was the next-to-last resting place of the first bishop of Florida, Bishop Verot, and concurrently, Father Varela, the Cuban patriot and prospective saint. Both bodies were relocated—Father Varela to Cuba and Bishop Verot to the center of Tolomoto Cemetery.

In fact, the cemetery is a virtual who's who of Floridian lore. Ana Eduardo Hernandez Gibbs, the young first wife of Kingsley Beatty Gibbs, of the famous Kingsley Plantation on St. George Island, rests in Tolomato Cemetery. There is also Catalina Usina Llambias, who lived in what is now

The chapel at sunset, where "women in white" materialize.

part of the St. Augustine Historical Society's "Oldest House" complex. She died in 1886, after the cemetery was closed to burials. Her son, Joseph, fulfilled her dying wish and buried her illegally in the Tolomato Cemetery. He was hauled into court by local authorities, chastised and fined twenty-five dollars. Catalina, however, was not disinterred.

Less famous but most representative of the St. Augustine citizens who sleep in Tolomato is modest Gertrude Pons, whose 1786 burial record is the first recorded death in the famous cemetery. Written in Latin but roughly translated, it reads, "Gertrude Pons, wife of Andres Paceti and a faithful member of the Holy Mother Church, gave up her soul to God…As a poor woman she did not dispose of anything else."

The Tolomato Cemetery
The west side of Cordova Street
St. Augustine, Florida, 32084
http://www.tolomatocemetery.com

BIBLIOGRAPHY

Adams, William R. *St. Augustine and St. Johns County: A Historical Guide.* Sarasota, FL: Pineapple Press, 2009.

Andrew, Erica. Personal interview, Harry's Seafood Bar and Grille, September 9 2011.

Arana, Luis Rafael, and Albert Manucy. *The Building of Castillo de San Marcos.* Philadelphia, PA: Eastern National, 1977. Out of Print, available at the St. Augustine Historical Society.

Avino, Violette. Personal interview, Ripley's Believe It or Not! Museum, June 8, 2012.

Belleville, Bill. *River of Lakes: A Journey on Florida's St. Johns River.* Athens: University of Georgia Press, 2000.

———. *Salvaging the Real Florida: Lost and Found in the State of Dreams.* Gainesville: University Press of Florida, 2011.

Bowen, Beth Rogero. *St. Augustine in the Gilded Age.* Charleston, SC: Arcadia Publishing, 2008.

Bronson, Bertrand Harris. *The Ballad as Song.* Berkeley: University of California, 1969.

Brown, C.H. "City Gate, Orange Street, Saint Augustine, St. Johns, FL." Historic American Buildings Survey. Washington, D.C.: Library of Congress, 1934. http://hdl.loc.gov/loc.pnp/hhh.fl0201.

Brown, Terry. "First Road to Freedom Led South to St. Augustine." *Florida Times-Union*, February 17, 2007.

Brown, Tom. Personal interview, Scarlett O'Hara's Bar and Restaurant, June 8, 2012.

Bullock, James. "Interview with James Bullock, Author of Freedom Road." By Matt Jeffs. *Airborne with Matt Jeffs*, 88.5 FM, Flagler College Radio, St. Augustine, Florida, 2007.

Burt, Al. *Becalmed in the Mullet Latitudes: Al Burt's Florida*. Port Salerno: Florida Classics Library, 1983.

Cain, Suzy, and Martin O'Shaughnessy. *A Ghostly Experience: Tales of St. Augustine*. [St. Augustine, FL]: Tour Saint Augustine, 1997.

Carlson, Charlie. *Weird Florida: Your Travel Guide to Florida's Local Legends and Best Kept Secrets*. New York: Barnes & Noble, 2005.

Cohen, Myer M. *Notices of Florida and the Campaigns*. New York: Burges & Honour, 1836.

Colee Clan. "Descendants of George Colee & Tryphena Riz." Ancestry. com, June 11, 2012. http://freepages.genealogy.roots.ancestry. com/~donnasfamilyhistory/colee/gcolee.htm.

Coomes, Charles S. "Tolomato Cemetery." *El Escribano* 13 (October 1976): 4.

Corley, Lyn. "Battle for America." Stone-Cut without Hands. June 2, 2012. http://stonecutwithouthands.com/battle_for_america2.pdf.

Cox, Dale. "Old City Gates—St. Augustine, Florida." Explore Southern History, October 24, 2011. http://www.exploresouthernhistory.com/staugustinegate.html.

Deagan, Kathleen A., and Darcie A. MacMahon. *Fort Mose: Colonial America's Black Fortress of Freedom*. Gainesville: University Press of Florida, 1995.

Dennis, Carl. "Drugstore." *Callings*. New York: Penguin Poets, 2010.

De Quesada, A.M. *A History of Florida Forts: Florida's Lonely Outposts*. Charleston, SC: The History Press, 2006.

DiRienzo, Patty. *Florida: A Journey through Its Colorful Past*. Boulder, CO: Westcliffe Publishing, 2008.

Drysdale, Evelyn. "History of Ancient Coquina Fort Is Traced through Centuries." *St. Augustine Record*, July 4, 1937.

Edwards, Virginia. *Stories of Old St. Augustine*. St. Augustine, FL: C.F. Hamblen, 1973.

Emerson, Ralph Waldo. *Journals of Ralph Waldo Emerson, 1820–1872*. Vol. 5. Edited by Edward Waldo Emerson and Waldo Emerson Forbes. Boston: Houghton Mifflin, 1909.

Feagin, Jackie. "Athalia: A Woman of Mystery, Controversy, Charm." *St. Augustine Record*, January 22, 1989.

Fichter, George S., and George Cardin. *Floridians All*. Gretna, LA: Pelican Publishing Company, 1991.

Florida: A Guide to the Southernmost State. New York: Oxford University Press, 1956.

Florida Archaeology Guide for Northeast Florida. "Huguenot Cemetery: Coquina Preserving the Past." *Coquina Queries,* September 17, 2011. http://www.fpannortheast.org/coquinaqueries.

Florida Humanities Council Forum 35, no. 3. "How Seashells Saved St. Augustine" (Fall 2011): 10.

Florida State Parks. *Fort Mose Historic State Park Audio Guide.* Cassette, recorded October 8, 2011.

Florida Times-Union. "Element of Time Puzzling in Trial." February 1, 1975, Jacksonville Journal section.

Fort Matanzas National Monument. *Fort Matanzas, Barrier Islands: The Changing Landscape of Fort Matanzas.* Washington, D.C.: National Park Service, U.S. Department of the Interior, 2002.

———. *Fort Matanzas: Great Horned Owl.* Washington, D.C.: National Park Service, U.S. Department of the Interior, 2011.

Fort Mose Historical Society. "Chronology of Fort Mose Events." 2006. http://www.fortmose.org/history/timeline.html.

Gannon, Michael. *Rebel Bishop: Augustin Verot, Florida's Civil War Prelate.* Gainesville: University Press of Florida, 1997.

Graham, Thomas. *Flagler's St. Augustine Hotels: The Ponce De Leon, the Alcazar, and the Casa Monica.* Sarasota, FL: Pineapple Press, 2004.

Guinta, Peter. "City Was End of Road to Freedom." *St. Augustine Record,* May 29, 2010.

———. "A Recurring Horror." *St. Augustine Record,* January 29, 2007.

———. "Three Parts of the Old Cubo Line Uncovered." *St. Augustine Record,* June 21, 2005.

Harvey, Karen G. *Oldest Ghosts: St. Augustine Haunts.* Sarasota, FL: Pineapple Press, 2000.

Harvey, Karen G., and Marianne Lerbs. *Five Women, Five Stories.* St. Augustine, FL: Dynamic Living, 2008.

Haskins, Lola. *Fifteen Florida Cemeteries: Strange Tales Unearthed.* Gainesville: University of Florida, 2011.

Hauck, Dennis William. *The National Directory of Haunted Places.* Sacramento, CA: Athanor, 1994.

Herbine, Sue. "Otto Curtis Lightner." Find-a-Grave, Ancestry.com, November 20, 2011.

Historic St. Augustine Preservation Board. Florida Master Site File Inventory Forms for 7 Aviles Street. Historic Properties Inventory Form, 1978.

———. Florida Master Site File Inventory Forms for 70 Hypolita Street. Historic Properties Inventory Form, 1978.

Hunt, Bruce. *Visiting Small-town Florida*. Sarasota, FL: Pineapple Press, 1997.

Hyman, Ann. "Book Revisits Unsolved St. Augustine Murder." *Florida Times-Union*, December 13, 1998.

Jenkins, Greg. *Florida's Ghostly Legends and Haunted Folklore*. Vol. 2. Sarasota, FL: Pineapple Press, 2005.

Kornwolf, James D., and Georgiana Wallis Kornwolf. *Architecture and Town Planning in Colonial North America*. Baltimore, MD: Johns Hopkins University Press, 2002.

Landers, Jane. *Colonial Plantations and Economy in Florida*. Gainesville: University Press of Florida, 2000.

———. "An Eighteenth-Century Community in Exile: The Floridanos in Cuba." *New West Indian Guide* (1996).

———. *Fort Mose: Gracia Real de Santa Teresa de Mose: A Free Black Town in Spanish Colonial Florida*. St. Augustine, FL: St. Augustine Historical Society, 1992.

Lane, Diane. "The Legend of the Love Tree." Produced by Love Tree Café, St. Augustine, 2012.

Lapham, Dave. *Ghosthunting in Florida*. Cincinnati, OH: Clerisy, 2010.

Lapham, Dave, and Tom Lapham. *Ancient City Hauntings: More Ghosts of St. Augustine*. Sarasota, FL: Pineapple Press, 2004.

Lightner Museum. "Highlights from the Collection." November 20, 2011. http://www.lightnermuseum.org/collect_lightner.html.

Louis Comfort Tiffany, the Morse Museum, Orlando, Florida. "The Charles Hosmer—Morse Museum of American Art." September 9, 2011. http://www.morsemuseum.org.

Martin, C. Lee. *Florida Ghosts and Pirates: Jacksonville, Fernandina, Amelia Island, St. Augustine, Daytona*. Atglen, PA: Schiffer Publishing, 2008.

Mason, Alana. Personal interview, Flagler College, September 9, 2011.

Mayhew, Augustus. "Oil Swells: The Standard Oil Crowd in Palm Beach." *New York Social Diary*, June 12, 2012. http://www.newyorksocialdiary.com/node/1904526.

Mitchel, Paul. "Key Question: Where Was Stanford?" *St. Augustine Record*, January 25, 1975.

Moffett, Langston. "About the Town." *St. Augustine Record*, April 30, 1944. Letter from Marjorie Kinnan Rawlings.

Nolan, David. *Fifty Feet in Paradise: The Booming of Florida*. San Diego, CA: Harcourt Brace Jovanovich, 1984.

————. *The Houses of St. Augustine*. Sarasota, FL: Pineapple Press, 1995.

Our Lady of Guadalupe. "The Apparitions and the Miracle." April 4, 2012. http:www.sancta.org/nican.html.

Outland, Sharon. St. Johns County Property Appraiser's Office raw data, Lightner Museum, St. Augustine, 2011.

Ovid. *Metamorphoses I–IV*. Edited by D.E. Hill. Warminster, Wiltshire, UK: Aris & Phillips, 1985.

Parker, Susan. "Unmarked Graves from St. Augustine's Early Years Lie Around Our Old Town." *St. Augustine Record*, February 24, 2002.

Philpot, J.H. *The Sacred Tree, or the Tree in Religion and Myth*. London: Macmillan and Company, 1897.

Pope, Margo C. "The Abbie Brooks Saga." *St. Augustine Record*, November 12, 2000, Sunday edition.

Powell, Jack. *Haunting Sunshine*. Sarasota, FL: Pineapple Press, 2001.

Powell, Nancy. "Socialite's Slaying Still Unsolved in St. Augustine." *Florida Times-Union*, November 23, 1976, Jacksonville Journal section.

Puterbaugh, Parke, and Alan Bisbort. *Moon Florida Beaches: The Best Places to Swim, Play, Eat, and Stay*. Emeryville, CA: Avalon Travel, 2006.

Rajtar, Steve. *A Guide to Historic St. Augustine, Florida*. Charleston, SC: The History Press, 2007.

Rep. Division of Recreation and Parks, State of Florida Department of Environmental Protection. *Fort Mose Historic State Park Unit Management Plan*. Tallahassee, FL: self-published, 2005.

"The Residents of 'Ribera Gardens Excavation' Area." Research notes, University of Florida George A. Smathers Libraries, Historic St. Augustine, Box 5, Block 12, Lots 26–28, Folder B12-L26, 27.

Russo, Harry. "Identity of Slayer Remains Controversial." *St. Augustine Record*, January 23, 1989.

————. "Murder Memories Still Scar." *St. Augustine Record*, January 22, 1989.

Saint Johns County, Florida Cemetery Records: St. Augustine, Evergreen Cemetery, Huguenot Cemetery, Jewish Cemetery, LaLaeche Shrine Cemetery, Moultrie Cemetery, San Lorenzo Catholic Cemetery, Yelvington Cemetery. Salem, MA: Higginson Book, 1998.

Singer, Steven D. *Shipwrecks of Florida*. Sarasota, FL: Pineapple, 1992.

St. Augustine Evening Record. "Death, Mrs. Charlotte Carcaba." March 17, 1924, 4.

————. "Inquest in Carcaba Case Was Held Friday." April 21, 1917, 1+.

————. "Romance Stirs in Anonymous Local Verses." July 4, 1937.

————. "W.H. Carcaba Was Shot and Killed Last Night." April 20, 1917, 1+.

St. Augustine Evening Star. "Laid to Rest: Body of Wm H. Carcaba Consigned to Grave Sunday Afternoon." April 24, 1917, 4.

St. Augustine Historical Society Research Library. *Tolomato Cemetery, Lists of Deaths and/or Burials.* Cemetery records, 1800–1899. St. Augustine, Florida.

St. Augustine Links Business Directory. "O.C. White's Restaurant—St. Augustine Florida—Seafood and Spirits." Window Path Services, November 27, 2011. http://www.ocwhitesrestaurant.com.

St. Augustine, Ponte Verde and the Beaches Visitors and Convention Bureau. "18th Annual Night of Lights Event Set for Nation's Oldest City." June 6, 2012. http://www.floridahistoriccoast.com/nights-of-lights/about.php.

St. Augustine Record. "Coroner's Jury Renders Verdict in Hotel Fire." April 20, 1944.

———. "Fire at Castle Warden Hotel Takes Lives of Popular Local Woman and Jacksonville Girl." April 24, 1944.

———. "First Hospital Established in This Old City." 1935.

———. "Miguel Ysnardy Was Builder of Worth Mansion." July 4, 1937.

———. "Rites Held for Mrs. Pickering at 4 Yesterday." April 26, 1944.

Stavely, John F. *Ghosts and Gravestones in St. Augustine, Florida.* St. Augustine, FL: Historic Tours of America, 2004.

St. Johns County Court Cases. *Eduardo F. Carcaba v. Lottie Carcaba.* Civil Action Case #1395, Court Document Cat. No. 112-18 Civil Action, 1917.

———. *Florida v. Lottie Carcaba and Victor White.* Court Document Cat. No. 182-60, 188-79, 1917.

———. *Lottie Carcaba Re: Habeas Corpus.* Case #857, Court Document Cat. No. 10-29, Civil, 1917.

———. *Lottie Carcaba v. Barbara and William Carcaba.* Case #714, Court Document Cat. No. 103-46, 47, Civil, Bill of Complaint, 1916.

———. *Lottie Carcaba v. William H. Carcaba.* Case #715, Court Document Cat. No. 103-49, Civil Cases, Divorce, 1916.

———. *St. Johns County Inquests William H. Carcaba.* Court Document Cat. No. 183-81, Civil Cases. 1917.

———. *William H. Carcaba v. Lottie Carcaba.* Case # 823, Court Document Cat. No. 11-37, Civil Case, Habeas Corpus for Custody of Children, 1916.

St. Johns County Property Appraisers Office raw data. Property Information, Official Records, 19 San Marcos, St. Augustine, Florida.

Strickland, Sandy. "74 Slaying Still Stirs Emotions." *Florida Times-Union,* January 31, 2000.

Sundin, Shawna. "Fort Mose Complex to Tell of Its History." *Florida Times-Union*, March 26, 2003.

Swanton, John Reed. *Early History of the Creek Indians and Their Neighbors*. Washington, D.C.: Government Printing Office, 1922.

Sweet, Frank W. *The Invasion of Spanish Florida*. Palm Coast, FL: Backintyme, 2000.

Traveler 23. "History Lives in City's Old House" (May 1979): 9.

University of Florida Institutional Repository, Florida Papers. "Tolomato Cemetery—Miguel Ysnardy v. Roman Catholic Church Proceedings." Archival edition, 1799.

Walch, Barbara H. *Frank B. Butler: Lincolnville Businessman and Founder of St. Augustine, Florida's Historic Black Beach*. St. Augustine, FL: R.B. Hadley Sr., 1992.

Willingham, Ben H., and Jeffrey L. Sizemore, eds. *Florida in Turmoil: The Terrible War Years, 1861–1865*. Jacksonville, FL: Museum of Southern History, 2011.

Wilson, Gil. "Alcazar Hotel of St. Augustine Florida." History of St. Augustine, November 23, 2011. http://www.drbronsontours.com/bronsonalcazar.html.

———. "2nd Spanish Period 1784–1821." History of St. Augustine, February 29, 2012. http://www.drbronsontours.com/bronsonhistorypagesecondspanish.html.

Winter, Nevin O. *Florida, the Land of Enchantment*. N.p.: Page Company, First Impression, 1918.

W.J. Harris Company, under the auspices of the St. Augustine Historical Society. "Souvenir of St. Augustine under Three Flags: Pictorial History of St. Augustine." February 3, 2012. http://www.augustine.com/history/PDF/under_three_flags.pdf.

ABOUT THE AUTHOR AND PHOTOGRAPHER

Bob and Elizabeth Randall are a husband and wife photojournalist team. Their most recent publication was a book about education titled *The Floating Teacher: A Guide to Surviving and Thriving.* Bob is a published freelance photographer and a business owner of a car stereo repair shop and a car stereo website. Elizabeth is a widely published freelance writer and a high school English teacher. They live in Lake Mary, Florida, with their daughter, Courtney.